Book — Made to Crave

See  W9-BCW-824

"Bill Mowry's book is an incredible tool for teaching the principles of doing life together. There is so much more to discipleship than just the content; it is rooted in relationships. This book puts the process of life2life discipleship in the reach of anyone willing to use it."

—TODD PETTY, senior pastor, Hillside Discipleship, Lapeeer, Michigan

"*The Ways of the Alongsider* is a practical, effective, and user-friendly resource for making disciples. Its usefulness is shown in the diversity of its application. People have been helped in such diverse settings as an inner-city church, with women, and with business entrepreneurs. I'm personally using it in international, cross-cultural settings. I couldn't recommend the material more."

—SAM HERSHEY, international director, Church Discipleship Ministry, The Navigators

"I have found *The Ways of the Alongsider* to be a profound tool to show experienced believers how they can be engaged in people's lives. The teaching framework and the tools truly help someone paint a new and tangible picture of doing ministry."

—DENNIS BLEVINS, national directors team member, Church Discipleship Ministry, The Navigators

"Our church used *The Ways of the Alongsider* in small groups. The greatest impact the material has made is on relationships. It has motivated our faith community to walk alongside each other in a more intentional discipleship-like manner, and this has changed people's lives."

—BEAU MCCARTHY, lead pastor, Genesis: The Church, Royal Oak, Michigan

"*The Ways of the Alongsider* has ignited a new passion for discipleship among our people. We have learned that making disciples is not a program for skilled professionals; it means simply coming alongside people and intentionally ministering life2life. *The Ways of the Alongsider* is one of the best discipleship tools I've used in a long time. It is biblical, simple, and reproducible. People's lives have been changed through a fresh encounter with Christ, and they are eager to pass it on to others."

—JAY JACKSON, team lead, Apex Church, Kettering, Ohio

"One of my core values is multiplying disciples. The teachings and strategies found in *The Ways of the Alongsider* have really enabled me to tackle this task with clarity and vision."

—DERRICK HURST, missions pastor, Atonement Lutheran Church, Columbus, Ohio

"I find with established Christians that *The Ways of the Alongsider* is the book to start with. It challenges church people out of complacency and stagnation into robust celebration. This is the greatest tool ever for Nav staff anytime, anywhere!"

—BOB FINSTROM, Church Discipleship Ministry, The Navigators

BILL MOWRY

THE Ways OF THE Alongsider

Growing Disciples Life2Life

NAVPRESS
Discipleship Inside Out®

CDM™
CHURCH DISCIPLESHIP MINISTRY

Discipleship Inside Out®

NavPress is the publishing ministry of The Navigators, an international Christian organization and leader in personal spiritual development. NavPress is committed to helping people grow spiritually and enjoy lives of meaning and hope through personal and group resources that are biblically rooted, culturally relevant, and highly practical.

**For a free catalog go to www.NavPress.com
or call 1.800.366.7788 in the United States or 1.800.839.4769 in Canada.**

© 2012 by William J. Mowry

www.alongsider.com

All rights reserved. No part of this publication may be reproduced in any form without written permission from NavPress, P.O. Box 35001, Colorado Springs, CO 80935. www.navpress.com

NAVPRESS and the NAVPRESS logo are registered trademarks of NavPress. Absence of ® in connection with marks of NavPress or other parties does not indicate an absence of registration of those marks.

ISBN-13: 978-1-61291-311-7

Cover design by Arvid Wallen
Cover illustration by Shutterstock/andesign101
Author photo by Marissa Mowry

Some of the anecdotal illustrations in this book are true to life and are included with the permission of the persons involved. All other illustrations are composites of real situations, and any resemblance to people living or dead is coincidental.

Unless otherwise identified, all Scripture quotations in this publication are taken from the *Holy Bible, New International Version®* (NIV®). Copyright © 1973, 1978, 1984 by Biblica, used by permission of Zondervan. All rights reserved. Other versions used include: the New American Standard Bible® (NASB), copyright © 1960, 1962, 1963, 1968, 1971, 1972, 1973, 1975, 1977, 1995 by The Lockman Foundation. Used by permission; the *Revised Standard Version Bible* (RSV), copyright © 1946, 1952, 1971, by the Division of Christian Education of the National Council of the Churches of Christ in the USA, used by permission, all rights reserved; *THE MESSAGE* (MSG). Copyright © 1993, 1994, 1995, 1996, 2000, 2001, 2002. Used by permission of NavPress Publishing Group; the *Amplified Bible* (AMP), © The Lockman Foundation 1954, 1958, 1962, 1964, 1965, 1987; and The Holy Bible, English Standard Version (ESV), copyright © 2001 by Crossway Bibles, a division of Good News Publishers, used by permission, all rights reserved.

Printed in the United States of America

2 3 4 5 6 7 8 / 17 16 15 14 13

This book is dedicated to my late mentor and friend, John Ed Robertson. John was the ultimate alongsider, teaching me that most of discipleship is "sticking with people until they get it." He stuck with me until I got it. Thanks, John Ed! Eternity will be populated with men and women you were an alongsider with.

disciple – <u>head</u>
knows who Christ is and made a decision to follow Him.
    – heart level – being Changed by Jesus
    – <u>hand</u> – Committed to mission of Christ
       (service) – makes new disciples

Jesus mission – make disciples

Contents

INTRODUCTION 9

Part One: Foundations

CHAPTER ONE The Way of the Amateur *Alongsiders do it from love.* 13

mark of alongsider ministry

CHAPTER TWO The Way of Life *Alongsiders minister from a friendship with God.* 21

Great Comission

CHAPTER THREE The Way of Intentionality *Alongsiders think big but start small.* 29

CHAPTER FOUR The Way of Prayer *Alongsiders partner with the Holy Spirit through prayer.* 39

Pray wisdom, protection, character, etc. into them. We can't, but Jesus can change them.

Part Two: Skills

CHAPTER FIVE The Way of Relationships *Alongsiders build authentic friendships.* 47

CHAPTER SIX The Way of Depth *Alongsiders go deep in relationships.* 57

CHAPTER SEVEN The Way of the Word *Alongsiders help others love and live the Scriptures.* 65

CHAPTER EIGHT The Way of Discovery *Alongsiders ask questions, tell stories, and encourage application.* 75

CHAPTER NINE The Way of Conversation *Alongsiders initiate purposeful conversations.* 85

CHAPTER TEN The Way of Mission *Alongsiders recruit people to live as insiders.* 95

WHAT DO I DO NEXT? 103

MY PLEDGE TO BE AN ALONGSIDER 105

Appendices

APPENDIX A The 5x5x5 Plan to Read the Bible 107

APPENDIX B Ten Ways to Recharge Your Daily Appointment with God 109

APPENDIX C Putting First Things First 111

APPENDIX D The Alongsider Circle 113

Welcome to the adventure of the alongsider.

It's time to clear away the clutter. Whether we're pastors, plumbers, accountants, or stay-at-home moms, our lives and ministries can get so cluttered that we miss out on the important. In church life, the clamor of competing demands can drown out the importance of making disciples. *The Ways of the Alongsider* will help clear out the clutter and get to the important.

The Ways of the Alongsider is more than a book to read; it's a life to experience. It is more than a program to complete; it's a passion to pursue. What's so different about this book? Much is written about the curriculum and content of discipleship, but relatively few writers tell us how to make disciples. This study guide will help you understand the ways and principles needed to help people become wholehearted followers of Jesus. Small-group leaders, parents, youth workers, teachers, and pastors will learn new ways to disciple others. I want you to finish this book and say, "By faith, I can do this. God can use me to make disciples!"

Let me be honest: I want to change how you think about disciplemaking. How will this happen? I want to change the picture you have of a disciplemaker. If the picture is changed, then the practices will change. What's the new picture? The following chapters will unveil a new image of disciplemaking. You will reflect on the life of Jesus and the instruction of the New Testament to discover the effective ways of an alongsider. This study guide is packed with Bible studies, personal reflection exercises, and practical assignments to provide the "how" of discipling others.

You will notice that this book is divided into two sections. The first section describes the **foundations** of the alongsider ministry—the ways of the amateur, of life, of intentionality, and of prayer. These foundations undergird the life and ministry of a disciplemaker. The next section portrays the simple ways or **skills** of an alongsider—how to build friendships, read the Bible with another, ask questions and encourage application, start purposeful conversations, and live on mission. These essential skills mark the practices of the alongsider.

The goal of this material is not just to read about disciplemaking but to actually begin making disciples. Your experience will be short-lived if you only read but don't apply what you discover. As you work your way through this book, you will be asked to prayerfully form an alongsider's circle of relationships. Begin to pray now for God to lead you to those eager men and women whom you can be an alongsider to.

I'm praying for God to raise up an ever-growing movement of alongsiders who are living the Great Commission right where they live, work, play, or worship. These alongsiders are committed to relational strategies—making disciples one conversation, one relationship at a time. Welcome to the adventure of the alongsider.

Part One:

Foundations

CHAPTER ONE

The Way of the Amateur

Alongsiders do it from love.

Introduction

A new neighbor moved into a house across the street from my parents. Within a few days, my father walked across the street to meet him. Dad soon discovered that the neighbor, Jack, was a widower and had lung cancer. Over time, my father initiated a faith conversation with him. Recognizing a need, my mother took over meals and Dad did some odd jobs for Jack. My parents invited him to their home Bible study and then to church. Jack came once to both events.

> In one recent nationwide survey we asked people to describe their goals in life. Almost nine of the ten adults describe themselves as "Christian.". . .
> But not one of the adults we interviewed said that their goal in life was to be a [disciple] or to make disciples. —George Barna

"I think he didn't come back because he was self-conscious about coughing and spitting up stuff," my dad said. Jack trusted Christ before he passed away from cancer.

The neighbor wasn't a project to my parents. They didn't love Jack because of their church's witnessing program. Mom and Dad were good neighbors because they believed that's what Jesus' disciples do. In the shadows of daily life in a mobile home park, my parents' lives won a neighbor's heart. They modeled 1 Thessalonians 5:12, living in the quiet, earning an "outsider's" respect. This respect birthed faith conversations.

Were the faith conversations haphazard? No, my father had received training in how to share his testimony and how to communicate the gospel. Were my parents retired ministry professionals? No, my dad was a meat cutter and my mother had worked in the school cafeteria. At nearly eighty years old, my parents were still bearing fruit. You could call them **ministry amateurs**.

As ministry amateurs they demonstrated a simple, relational strategy. Walk across the street, befriend a neighbor, start some faith conversations, and trust God to do the rest. We don't need larger buildings, costly programs, or more church staff to do this. We just need to disciple and release people to love others right where they live, work, or play. Imagine the impact if we had scores of men and women like my parents—people committed to this simple, relational strategy—doing the Great Commission one conversation, one relationship at a time.

God is looking for ministry amateurs.

God is looking for amateurs to make disciples. This should be an encouragement to anyone wanting to participate in the Great Commission. In the original meaning of the word, amateurs are not people who lack skill or training. The word *amateur* comes from the Latin word meaning "lover." Amateurs are often skilled people working without compensation. Amateurs work not for pay but out of the sheer love and joy of what they do.

The Apostles were ministry amateurs. When Jewish boys reached their mid-teens, the best and the brightest were recruited by the local rabbi for advanced study. For those who didn't qualify, apprenticeship in a vocation was the next step. More fishermen were always needed (Matthew 4:21-22). These religious amateurs (the Apostles) created a stir. When the ministry professionals observed their boldness and confidence, they were amazed because "they were uneducated, common men . . . and they recognized that they had been with Jesus" (Acts 4:13, ESV).

The early church was a movement of amateurs. Church historian Michael Green writes, "The great mission of Christianity [in converting the Roman Empire] was in reality accomplished by means of informal missionaries. . . . They did it naturally, enthusiastically, and with the conviction of those who are not paid to say that sort of thing."[1] God wants to use ministry amateurs.

> Jesus aimed to start a movement which would reach the whole world. He had three years in which to do it. And He deliberately devoted Himself to twelve men. . . . It occurred to me that such a strategy could not be improved upon.
> —Richard Halverson

Why do we disqualify ourselves, believing we have to be ministry professionals to make disciples? I think it's because of the pictures we hang in our minds about disciplemaking. Too often, we picture disciplemaking taking place in a classroom with a gifted teacher. We think, "I could never make disciples because I'm not a teacher." Another picture we hang in our minds is a complex image of standards and qualifications. One popular disciplemaking book lists thirty topics to cover in discipling another. *These thirty qualities are not in my life!* we say to ourselves. *How can I ever make a disciple?*

Jesus does the unthinkable. He invites us, in our weakness and inexperience, to be His helpers in the Great Commission. He recruits ministry amateurs to come alongside friends to model behaviors—such as how to love God, build friendships, read the Bible with others, tell stories, ask questions—and encourage application. We could call these amateur disciplemakers **alongsiders**.

The ministry of the alongsider

Author Warren Wiersbe writes, "No Christian rises higher than the beauty and quality of the pictures that hang in the gallery of his or her mind."[2] Ministering as an alongsider means hanging a new picture of disciplemaking in our minds. Instead of the word *disciplemaker*, let's hang the picture of an alongsider. Alongsiders are ministry amateurs who come next to friends, helping them follow Christ.

The ministry of the alongsider comes from the Greek word *paraclesis*, meaning "a calling to one's side," "an active helper, or counselor."[3] The Holy Spirit is the ultimate alongsider, a Helper who is with us forever (John 14:16,26). Whom does the Holy Spirit use? Amateurs like us who come alongside friends to encourage, comfort, and exhort (Romans 15:14; 1 Thessalonians 2:11; 5:14).

The language and ministry of paraclesis is different from preaching (*kerugma*) and teaching (*didasko*). Preaching is directed toward the will, while teaching is directed to the mind. The ministry of paraclesis complements these two. Author Eugene Peterson describes it this way: "[Paraclesis] introduces a quieter, more conversational tone, something on the order of, 'I'm here at your side, let's talk this over, let's consider how we can get in on everything that God is doing.'"[4]

The alongsider practices the language of paraclesis, a language used with men and women who have received the Word, preached, and taught but now need help to apply it in the challenges of life. "Paracletic language is the language of the Holy Spirit, a language of relationships and intimacy, a way of speaking and listening that gets the words of Jesus inside us."[5] This paracletic ministry happens through alongsiders, people who choose to disciple others in life2life ways.

Alongsiders minister in life2life ways.

When I trusted Christ as a sophomore in college, I knew I should do three things: read the Bible, pray, and see Ed.

Ed was the guy who lived across the hall from me in my freshman dorm. After we first met, I discovered that he was a Christian. Even though I initially resisted Ed's "religious talk," we became best friends. His persistent witness drew me to the Savior. I knew that if I had questions about my new faith, I could trust Ed to be my guide.

When I told Ed about my faith commitment, he did something simple: He invited me to read the Bible with him in the dormitory study lounge. This began a habit of praying together, reading the Scriptures, debating our interpretations, and sharing our applications. This was life2life discipleship—two friends meeting over an open Bible, sharing their lives together, and helping one another follow Jesus.

I soon discovered that Ed followed Jesus' example. When the Lord invited His disciples to "be with him" (Mark 3:14), it meant joining the Lord in His life. Together, they went to social events, went on walking expeditions, enjoyed faith conversations, and shared in the joys and sorrows of ministry. Jesus was an alongsider, intentionally ministering life2life.

The Apostle Paul practiced a life2life approach. With the young Thessalonian church, he reminded them that he, Silas, and Timothy had shared not only the gospel but "also our own lives, because you

> Discipleship is not with the many but with the few and with the one. Disciplemaking is done in life2life ways and through alongsiders.

> Our most serious failure today is the inability to provide effective practical guidance as to how to live the life of Jesus.
> —Dallas Willard

had become very dear to us" (1 Thessalonians 2:8, NASB). Life2life ministry moves beyond explaining the gospel to entering into a friend's God-story.

My friend Ed entered into my God-story and imprinted me with a love for God. He taught me that helping others follow Jesus is more than mastering a curriculum or perfecting techniques. Discipleship is passing on a life in Christ from one person to another. In life2life ministry, relationships become the highway for spiritual transformation. I'm eternally grateful that Ed was an alongsider, taking time to live life2life with me.

Alongsiders disciple people in the middle.

We have unintentionally created a gap in the Christian life. We emphasize evangelism, encouraging personal conversion to Christ. The promise of conversion is a life lived in eternity (heaven). However, we can sometimes exclude the gap between conversion and eternity, life lived in the middle. This life in the middle happens between Sunday church services, where we live, work, study, or play. Author Lauren Winner notes that "faithfulness is about recognizing that most of my hours will be devoted to life in the middle."[6] Alongsiders know that discipleship is about what happens in the middle.

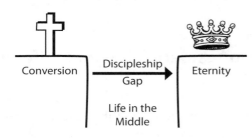

The Apostle Paul understood how life is lived in the middle when he exhorted the Philippians to live without blemish "in the midst of a crooked and twisted generation." Right in the middle of work, neighborhood, and family, we're to live "as lights in the world" (Philippians 2:15, ESV). The test of a disciple's life is not found in a worship service or a retreat but in the midst of a crooked generation. Alongsiders know that discipleship is about what happens in the middle.

Alongsiders hang new pictures.

The alongsider ministry takes down some traditional pictures. For starters, we take down our pictures of the classroom, study, or church sanctuary. These still have a place, but they're not as prominent. We now hang some new ones, pictures like the living room, a workplace, or a bleacher seat. All of life becomes a classroom for the alongsider. Instead of being the teacher, placed above students, we're companions on the journey (Matthew 23:8-12), purposefully coming alongside people to follow Christ together. To do this we must hang some new pictures.

When we minister as alongsiders, we earn the right to intentionally become involved in people's lives. Alongsiders partner with the Holy Spirit, helping others wholeheartedly follow Jesus in all of life. We purposefully do this in simple, life2life ways: loving one another, reading the Bible, telling stories, asking questions, encouraging application, and living on mission.

Hanging new pictures begins with evaluating how our traditional approaches to ministry compares with an alongsider's approach. While there's always room for traditional approaches, alongsiders take some alternate routes. Here's one way to illustrate the differences between the two.

Traditional approaches	The way of the alongsider
• classroom	• small group and one-to-one
• content and curriculum	• character and practice
• one-way (teacher to pupil)	• two-way (discovery and discussion)
• complete the course or curriculum	• live and practice life
• teach through a lecture	• teach people to study for themselves
• tell him or her how	• show him or her how
• information	• encourage transformation
• scheduled program	• lifestyle to live

Stop and reflect for a moment. In this box, describe your current picture of disciplemaking. Feel free to be creative and combine words with sketches.

Now ponder the ways of the alongsider when compared to traditional approaches. What would change about your picture? In this box, combine some words and sketches of this change.

Alongsiders apply VIM.

Living as an alongsider is highly relational but it is not haphazard. Like the Apostle Paul, we want to intentionally "present everyone mature in Christ" (Colossians 1:28, ESV). We aspire to be a "skilled master builder" (1 Corinthians 3:10, ESV), purposefully laying foundations in people's lives to help them follow Jesus.

One way to bring intentionality to the alongsider process is to apply VIM. VIM represents three elements: **V**ision, **I**ntentionality, and **M**eans. Vision is the motivation and desired end. Intentionality represents a purposeful approach. Means describes tools and resources to help. One author says that these three elements are "the general pattern for spiritual transformation" and the path for change.[7]

Vision	Do I have a picture or vision for change?
Intentional	Do I desire change? Have I decided to be intentional about change?
Means	Do I have the means (tools, practical helps, training) for change?

All three work in concert. If I have vision and intentionality without resources, my intentions may be good but they bear few results. If I have intentionality and resources without vision, I can major on methods without heart. All three are indispensable to the process.

Keep the VIM principle in mind as you come alongside people in their discipleship journey. VIM will challenge you to ask such questions as: What is your vision for discipleship? How are you encouraging intentionality for change? What practical tools or resources can be helpful to build in change? Sprinkled throughout the book are some VIM examples.

How would you rate your effectiveness as an alongsider?

This assessment evaluates your ability and commitment to disciple people through the ways of the alongsider. Rate each statement on a scale of one to five. One indicates that you seldom practice this behavior. Five indicates that you regularly practice this behavior. Total your scores at the end.

_3_ 1. I believe that effective disciplemaking flows from a healthy walk with God.

_4_ 2. I take time to learn a person's background and hear his or her faith story.

_5_ 3. I believe that our friendship is as important as the right curriculum.

_1_ 4. I seek to participate in common hobbies and social events.

_3_ 5. I develop specific goals that are tailor-made for each person.

_3_ 6. I look for others in the body of Christ who can contribute to people through their unique set of gifts and experiences.

_1_ 7. I invite people to join a small group for maximum impact.

_3_ 8. I spend one-to-one time with people to show them how to practically follow Christ.

_1_ 9. I come alongside and help people meditate and apply the Scriptures.

_5_ 10. I have a clear picture of a New Testament disciple.

_5_ 11. I set the example in transparency and vulnerability.

_3_ 12. I make every effort to model a life of discipleship.

_2_ 13. I do not depend on my abilities or techniques but intentionally trust God to change people through prayer.

_2_ 14. I visit my friend's place of work, home, or apartment.

_1_ 15. I seek to set the example of discipling others.

Total: _42_

1-25   I'm a beginner at being an alongsider.
26-55   I'm growing at being an alongsider.
56-75   I'm a skilled practitioner at being an alongsider.

What did you discover about your strengths as an alongsider?

What did you discover about some areas of growth for yourself as an alongsider?

Over the next few weeks, what would you like to strengthen in your ministry of being an alongsider?

2)

6) Find out who has the resources ...

8) Spend one on one time w/ someone

Over the next few weeks, what area of need would you like to turn into a strength?

— Study Bible more
— Pray more intentionally

CHAPTER TWO

The Way of Life

Alongsiders minister from a friendship with God.

Introduction

Have you ever discovered yourself driving a familiar route over and over again so often that you've stopped looking at the landscape? Boredom sets in and we no longer notice what is around us. The obvious becomes overlooked. The Bible can become a similar drive-by experience. Certain passages are so familiar that we stop looking. One example is the Great Commission passage, the charge to make disciples in Matthew 28:16-20. It's so familiar that we stop looking and miss foundational truth.

Matthew 28:16-20 describes the scene of eleven men meeting their risen Lord. What happened when they encountered Jesus? The obvious is that they listened to His command. What is not so obvious is that they worshipped Him first. This wasn't a typical worship service. No guitar was pulled out to lead in a chorus nor was an offering taken.

I picture a group of men kneeling in quiet adoration, raising their hands in wonder, or hugging their Lord because they missed Him. Worship, expressed in relationship, preceded the mission to make disciples. The eleven understood the way of life, a life lived in friendship with God. They didn't want this obvious truth to become neglected, and neither should we if we're to live as alongsiders.

Alongsiders practice a way of life that begins with a thirst for God. Author John Stott writes that Christians should be spiritual "dipsomaniacs"—people who are always thirsty for God.[1] King David recognized this thirst when he wrote,

> As a deer pants for flowing streams,
>   so pants my soul for you, O God.
> My soul thirsts for God,
>   for the living God.
> When shall I come and appear before God? (Psalm 42:1-2, ESV)

There's nothing more basic, and transformative, than walking in a close relationship with our Father. Alongsiders are convinced that their ministry flows from a rich friendship with God. Loving God is at the core of an alongsider's being.

David was heartsick. Ease he did not seek, honor he did not covet, but the enjoyment of communion with God was an urgent need of his soul. . . . His very self, his deepest life, was insatiable for a sense of the divine presence.
—Charles Spurgeon

If there's one devotional book that has challenged believers over the years, it's probably *My Utmost for His Highest* by Oswald Chambers. For nearly a century, Chambers' messages, distilled to daily readings, have nourished the souls of countless people. Chambers lived and preached what it meant to be a friend of God. Listen to his heart:

Before Pentecost the disciples knew Jesus as the One Who gave them power to conquer demons and to bring about a revival (Luke 10:18-20). It was a wonderful intimacy, but there was a much closer intimacy to come—"I have called you friends." Friendship is rare on earth. It means identity in thought and heart and spirit. The whole discipline of life is to enable us to enter this closest relationship with Jesus Christ.[2]

When we live as friends of God, we begin to experience the full and abundant life of Christ (John 10:10). This abundant life is an overflow of the Holy Spirit, welling up and spilling out of a renewed heart and mind (John 7:37-39). Without this life in Christ, we pass on rules and regulations, preferences and practices. Alongsiders minister from the abundant life that Christ provides through a friendship with Him.

We can be squeamish about referring to God as our friend. We fear making the Lord of the universe our celestial buddy, diminishing His majesty and holiness. This is a valid concern but not a reason to throw out the analogy. Author Eugene Peterson writes that "intimacy does not preclude reverence. True intimacy does not eliminate a sacred awe."[3] Jesus invites us to use the most intimate family term of "daddy" when we pray (Matthew 6:9). At the same time, we're to hallow and make sacred the name of our Father in heaven. He invites us into a paradoxical relationship of closeness and worship, friendship and obedience.

God is the ultimate alongsider.

1. One simple act describes friendship—friends come alongside friends. Our Lord is the ultimate alongsider. Describe from the following passages how our Father comes alongside of us.

- Psalm 34:18 *The Lord is near to those w/ 1) broken heart and 2) contrite spirit*

- Psalm 36:7 *Treats us w/ lovingkindness)*
  We put our trust under the shadow of your wings

Fear not,

- Isaiah 41:10   *I am with you ; I am your God.*
I will strengthen you, help you, uphold
you.

- Isaiah 57:15 *¹⁾ revives the spirit of the humble,*
² revives the heart of the contrite

- Matthew 1:23 *Promise of Jesus birth (Immanuel)*
"God with us"

- Matthew 28:20 *I am with you always, even to the*
end of the age.

Friendship is the noun that best fits fellowship with the Father and Son into which we were called. —J. I. Packer

In Proverbs 3:32, the writer describes how "the upright are in his confidence" (ESV). The word *confidence* (*intimate* in the NASB) means "private counsel." The Hebrew root means "to be tight, firm, pressed together." One of the derivatives for "confidence" is the word for pillows or cushions, which are pressed together on a bed or couch. Proverbs 3:32 portrays people being pressed together for the purpose of confidential communication. The word is used of lovers whose heads are pressed to each other on a pillow or friends sharing their thoughts while sitting close together on a couch.[4]

2. How would you describe God's role as an alongsider?

God's secret counsel is with the upright ; the perverse person
is an abomination to the Lord.
teacher, instructs, protects, loves, doesn't criticize, never leaves
me - always has my best interests
in mind.

3. Give an example of how the Lord came alongside of you.

- Peace + Comfort when marriage was falling apart.
- Jesus little lamb (holds me tenderly when I encounter probs.)

4. How can an understanding of God as an alongsider help you be an alongsider to others?

It encourages me to persevere thru thick 'n thin

Friendship is the mark of God's alongsider ministry.

5. Check the statement that comes closest to describing your friendship with God.

☐ The thought of being close to God is scary to me.
☐ I've never thought of God as my friend.
☐ I long for friendship and closeness with God, but I've never experienced them.
☐ I have experienced closeness with God during certain periods of my life, but not consistently.
☑ I experience a growing friendship with God most of the time.

6. Think back on those times when you felt closest to God. Describe the circumstances or conditions that caused you to be close to Him.

- Marriage was failing - arguing, needs not being met, distrust
- Feeling unloved in family - "the look"
- lack of positive feedback
- Manners - to - butler.

7. Read Exodus 33:11 and Numbers 12:8. How is Moses' relationship with God described?

Spoke face to face w/ the LORD, as a man speaks to his friend

The extraordinary unique, intimate relationship that Jesus himself had enjoyed with the Father is now open to all his followers. In the first of his resurrection chapters, John finally explains why and how this comes about. The risen Jesus tells Mary Magdalene to go and say to "my brothers," "I am going up to my Father and your Father, to my God and your God."
—N. T. Wright

- What do you think it means to speak to someone "face to face"?

  intimately — of things not shared w/ just anybody.

- How is this a sign of friendship?

  No fear - trust God w/ feelings & flaws.

- Do you think we can be friends with God in the same way as Moses? Why or why not? *Yes — spend more time in the Word & prayer.*

Charge Head, heart, hands level
Jesus mission on earth was to make disciples.
Great Commission: Matt. 28:16-20
John 1:1 "The Word" is Jesus - as an alongsider, pass that along to new
Christians.

8. Read Matthew 22:37-38. How does Jesus describe friendship with God?

Love him w/ all your heart, soul, mind.

• What happens to friendship when love is absent?

No depth = no trust

9. Read John 15:13-15. What does Jesus have to say about friendship?

Willing to die for a friend. Friend knows what the master is doing - not so w/ a servant. Jesus calls us friends.

• How does this add to your understanding of what it means to be a friend of God?

Jesus wants to make known (through the Word) all He has heard from the Father.

10. Read John 14:21. What does Jesus say about the person who loves Him?

- Will keep his commandments
- keeping the commandments will be loved by Jesus AND the Father.
- Jesus will manifest Himself to those who love Him.

• What do you think Jesus means when He says that He will show Himself to the one who obeys Him?

More of Jesus' character will be revealed
We'll become more like Jesus.

• Do you think showing yourself is a statement of friendship? Explain your answer.

Transparent leads to trust + greater more love

11. The Apostle Paul placed knowing God at the top of his priority list. The Amplified Bible translates Philippians 3:10 in this way:

[For my determined purpose is] that I may know Him [that I may progressively become more deeply and intimately acquainted with Him, perceiving and recognizing and understanding the wonders of His Person more strongly and more clearly].

- What can you learn from this passage about being a friend of God?

12. What are the qualities of a friend of God? Add to the following list.

A friend of God is one who:

- Practices a trust in Him
- Confides his or her deepest needs and anxieties to Him
- Looks forward to spending time with Him
- *Talks to Him (prayer)*
- *Thanks Him*   *• Loves Him in all circumstances*
  Loves Him

> Seeking intimacy with the Almighty requires focused attention.
> —Chuck Swindoll

13. Explain why you want to be a friend of God.

- be able to stand in that day
- become more like Him
- become more confident in who I am as His little girl
- be a better friend to others.

We come alongside God through a simple practice.

Across time and culture, God-thirsty people have practiced a simple discipline. It's been called a variety of names—daily watch, quiet time, daily devotional—but the principle is the same. We grow in our friendship with God when we come alongside Him through a daily time in His Word and prayer. When we establish a routine of daily appointments with God, we realize over time that something has happened in our relationship. We're now people experiencing "God-friendship," becoming "the ones he confides in" (Psalm 25:14, MSG).

14. Why is spending time with a friend critical in maintaining the relationship?

Too easy for the world to suck us into something else, we forget the other person. Loss of trust

15. True friendship is rooted in the heart. In Philippians 3:8, the Apostle Paul describes his heart for knowing Christ. Underline some of the key words describing Paul's motivation in knowing Christ.

> Yes, furthermore, I count everything as loss compared to the possession of the <u>priceless privilege</u> (the overwhelming preciousness, the surpassing worth, and <u>supreme advantage</u>) of knowing Christ Jesus my Lord and of progressively <u>becoming more deeply and intimately acquainted with Him</u>. . . . For His sake I have lost everything and consider it all to be mere rubbish (refuse, dregs) in order that <u>I may win</u> (gain) <u>Christ</u>. (AMP)

> Communion with God is so sweet that the chill of the morning is forgotten and the luxury of the couch despised.
> —Charles Spurgeon

• From this passage, how would you describe Paul's motivation for knowing Christ?

 Extreme! Would lose all to get to know Jesus.

• Paul counted some things as loss, or rubbish, for the surpassing worth of knowing Christ. What rubbish in your life do you need to discard in order to know Christ?

 Free up more time
 Don't succomb to temptation to shop for unnecessary "stuff"
 Set a regular quiet time w/ Jesus.

16. To become deeply and intimately acquainted with Christ, we put off some things and put on other things. One practice to put on is spending time with Him. From these passages, describe why spending time with our Lord is so important.

• Psalm 16:11   *joy + pleasures forever more.*

• Psalm 62:1-2   *from Him comes my salvation*
 He's my defense.   Confidence

• Jeremiah 31:3   *Experience His love*

• Mark 1:35   *He's our example:*
 early morning prayer was Jesus' habit.
 in solitary place

17. How would you rate your success in spending regular time with the Father?

❑ I'm not very motivated to maintain a daily appointment.
☒ I'm motivated but struggle with consistency.
❑ I'm consistent, but it's become routine rather than a joy.
❑ I'm motivated and regularly spend time with God.

Alongsiders do it with VIM.

V	I want to help people experience a life-changing friendship with God.
I	My desire to know God and a decision to practice a daily appointment with Him will turn this vision into reality.
M	A practical way to cultivate a friendship with God is through a daily appointment with Him. I will choose one of the practical tools to use in building a friendship with God through a daily appointment.

Alongsiders take action.

Whether you're a beginner or a frequent companion, we all need to refresh our times with the Father. Appendices A, B, and C provide practical tools for developing or deepening our appointments with God:

- Appendix A—The 5x5x5 Plan to Read the Bible
- Appendix B—Ten Ways to Recharge Your Daily Appointment with God
- Appendix C—Putting First Things First

Read all three appendices and choose one action to take this week.

This week, I will _____.

You can download several free resources to begin a daily appointment with God at www.navpress.com (go to the Alongsider page) or www.alongsider.com.

The Way of Intentionality

Alongsiders think big but start small.

Life w/ Jesus
I do, they watch
I do, they help
They do, I help
They do, I watch

Introduction

God enjoys reversing the order of things. Do you want to lead? Then choose the life of a servant. Do you want to live? Then you need to die. Do you want to impact the world? Then start small.

God delights in smallness. His kingdom is like a mustard seed, a misplaced coin, or a lost sheep. Jesus thought big about the world but started small, with only twelve men. Instead of recruiting to a program, He recruited people to a way of life.

> The word *disciple* occurs 269 times in the New Testament. . . . The New Testament is a book about disciples, by disciples, and for disciples of Jesus Christ.
> —Dallas Willard

Jesus' way is different from the culture around us. This difference is found in who we are—our devotion, our character, our identity, our mission—not in the clothes we wear, the politics we hold, or the activities we attend. Living Jesus' way is a change of life that begins from the inside out (John 3:3-5). This is His way to change the world.

When we examine Jesus' way of ministry, we discover that He didn't invest His time with the multitudes. He intentionally invested His energies with a select few. Jesus believed that quality would reproduce quantity. Following in the steps of the Master, the alongsider purposefully invests in a few people, who will then multiply into the world.

The way of intentionality goes against our usual standards of success. Let's be honest. We get more excited about how many people attend a meeting than how many are living Jesus' way. Less is more in Jesus' way of ministry. He knew that discipleship did not take place with the many but with the few and the one. Are you ready to think big by intentionally starting small?

Alongsiders learn from Jesus.

Read Mark 3:7-19 and reflect on the following questions.

1. How would you describe the public's response to Jesus' ministry? They all wanted to see Him and experience the miracles firsthand.

The Ways OF THE Alongsider

Book – Not a fan
There are followers
and there are fans.

2. Why do you think He intentionally chose a few (twelve) even as He continued a public ministry to ever-growing crowds?

Because they were the quality he wanted:
humble
sincere believers in Jesus

3. Mark writes that Jesus appointed twelve "that they might be with him" (verse 14). Why do you think being "with him" is so important for life2life disciplemaking?

We need Jesus' power & example with us
to model to others — share w/ others.

> One must decide where he wants his ministry to count—in the momentary applause of popular recognition or in the reproduction of his life in a few chosen men who will carry on his work after he has gone. Really it is a question of which generation we are living for.
> —Robert Coleman

4. Could Jesus have accomplished His mission (verse 14) by simply staying with the crowds? Why or why not?

He multiplied himself by choosing the
12 – "one candle lights one candle"

5. Jesus' decision to intentionally choose twelve disciples was made after nearly one and a half years of associating with these men. They had accompanied Jesus on ministry tours, shared in conversations, and observed the Master in ministry. Why do you think Jesus took so much time before making His choices?

To choose only those who had "what it takes"
to make disciples & fulfill Jesus' mission:
even Judas!

Alongsiders think big but start small.

6. Read Matthew 28:16-20 and reflect on the following meditation questions.

F = faithful
A = available ⎫ *We need to*
T = teachable ⎭ *find FAT people*
to start small

Be with = more info is caught than taught.

- Picture yourself as one of the eleven disciples with Jesus in Matthew 28:16-20. Of all the things our Lord could have said in His final instructions, why do you think He placed an emphasis on making more disciples? *So they'd reproduce more disciples and spread throughout the world.*

- Going to all the nations would have challenged this small band of eleven men. Bruxy Cavey writes,

  Jesus' message of God's love was radically inclusive in a world where religions were anything but. Ancient religions were tribal, defined by ethnic and political boundaries. Different people groups, nationalities, and city-states all worshiped their own god or gods. These deities would, not surprisingly, support the cultural and political agendas of the particular groups to which they belonged.[1]

  With this background, what do you think was going through the minds of the disciples when Jesus charged them to go to all the nations? *How will we break through the barriers of false gods?*

- In what ways did Jesus think big by starting small?
  Small would be able to impact one life at a time (non-threatening in a idol worshipping exclusive culture.)

7. In *The Master Plan of Evangelism*, author Robert Coleman gives additional insight into Matthew 28:18-20:

  The mission is emphasized even more when the Greek text of the passage is studied, and it is seen that the words "go," "baptize," and "teach" are all participles which derive their force from the one controlling verb "make disciples." This means that the great commission is not merely to go to the ends of the earth preaching the gospel nor to baptize a lot of converts in the Name of the Triune God, nor to teach them the precepts of Christ, but to make disciples.[2]

• What insight does Coleman provide about the central meaning of verses 18-20?

Go, baptize, teach are all part of make disciples

• Author Bill Hull writes, "'Going' is a circumstantial participle that could be understood to mean, 'as you are going.' Therefore, as you are going through life, whether you travel or live a localized life, this work is for you."[3] What insights does this statement add to the imperative of making disciples?

Nobody is exempt because of where you live, what you do, or how much money (resources) you have.

8. Remember how we're changing the pictures that hang in our minds? At this moment, how would you describe your mind's picture about the Great Commission? Check the ones that most apply.

❏ I could never see myself making disciples.
❏ I think I could make disciples, but I really lack confidence.
☒ I would like to make disciples, but I need some additional growth.
☒ I would like to make disciples, but I need some additional training.
❏ I'm ready to go and make disciples!

9. Read Matthew 28:16-20 again. How would you describe the emotional state of the disciples when they met Jesus on the mountain? Do you think they felt ready?

*Fearful — not feeling ready.
"some doubted"*

Jesus addressed these concerns by placing two "bookends" around the command to make disciples. "All authority . . . has been given to me" and "I am with you always" surround, or bookend, the command to make disciples. Nowhere else does He make these statements regarding a command. How can these two assurances help meet our fears and apprehensions in making disciples? What can they do to change our mental pictures of disciplemaking?

*If God (Jesus) is for us, who can be against us?
He is with us — no need to fear.*

Alongsiders think in generations.

God sees the world through the lives of individuals. The Bible is peppered with individual personalities. We know them as Abraham, Job, Ruth, David, Mary, and Martha. Each individual has the potential to influence countless others for Christ. This influence is often pictured in generations.

10. Read Psalm 78:1-8. Count the number of generations in this passage and complete the following illustration.

Jacob ⟶ Israel ⟶ *all the world*

- Why do you think the author focuses on future generations rather than only the present generation?

  That's how God chose to do it from the beginning of time. If not, stubborn & rebellious people will propagate that to their kids!

11. Spiritual generations are at the heart of Jesus' prayer in John 17. What can you learn about generations from John 17:6,20-23?

    They will believe in Jesus through our word. Jesus is praying for the believer — present and future believers.

> When Jesus said, "Make disciples," by necessity, the disciples understood it to mean much more than simply getting people to believe in Jesus. They had seen hundreds come and go; had witnessed the multitudes of the needy, the takers, and the superficial scramble after the spectacular; and knew that getting people to say, "Yes, I believe," was not enough.
> —Bill Hull

12. The Apostle Paul had generations on his heart as he neared the end of his life. What can you learn about generations from 2 Timothy 2:2? How many generations are described in this passage? *One at a time*

- When we minister as alongsiders, we see the world through individuals. If we're not building quality into the lives of people, what will happen to future generations?

  watered down — lose sight of reality.

Alongsiders are intentional.

Did you know that the early followers of Jesus were called people of "the Way" before they were called Christians (Acts 9:2)? It all started with Jesus' pronouncement in John 14:6. When Jesus refers to Himself as "the way and the truth and the life," this was more than a way (means) to salvation but a way (lifestyle) of living.

When we ask someone to "look at the way I do this" or "do it my way," we're describing a model or "way" of doing things. When Jesus invites us to follow Him as His disciples, He's inviting us to a way of living. Those who identify with Jesus as His disciples will have a certain way about them.

Jesus addressed this theme in Matthew 28:18-20. *The Message* translation puts it this way:

> God authorized and commanded me to commission you: Go out and train everyone you meet, far and near, in this way of life, marking them by baptism in the threefold name. . . . Then instruct them in the practice of all I have commanded you.

A disciple in the New Testament primarily means a "follower," "imitator," or "learner."[4] When a rabbi asked someone to follow him, it was more than a casual relationship. This was an intentional commitment to learn from a master. In Jesus' use of the word, it meant more than mastering His teachings. Discipleship for Jesus meant a decision on the part of the learner to allow His teachings to shape and transform his or her life. Living out Jesus' teaching translates into a way of life. Discipleship describes a lifetime quest to intentionally learn and live the ways of Jesus in the here and now.

13. Do you think every believer is automatically a disciple of Jesus? Why or why not?

No – start as babies & keep learning.

14. What mental picture do you have of a disciple of Jesus? Write a simple description of a disciple.

Do as he commanded – reproduce yourself.

15. A clear picture of a disciple hung in Jesus' mind. This picture formed a bull's-eye for His ministry. Jesus did not leave disciplemaking to chance but intentionally focused His energies toward a picture of maturity. Without a bull's-eye, we shoot our discipleship arrows randomly and miss the target.

What are the ways of Jesus' disciples? Read the following groupings of verses and summarize in one or two sentences the ways of a disciple. The first one is illustrated for you. Enjoy the challenge of discovering Jesus' picture of a disciple.

Matthew 22:37 / Philippians 3:8

The way of a disciple is to love God with my entire being, placing this love above everything else.

Luke 9:23 / Galatians 2:20

The way of a disciple is to deny selfish desires every day to follow (do) Jesus' will, to the point that it's no longer me that does Jesus' will, but Jesus himself.

John 13:34-35 / Hebrews 10:24-25

Love one another, do good works, meet together, exhorting one another

> The church is looking for better methods; God is looking for better men.
> —E. M. Bounds

John 8:31-32 / 2 Timothy 3:16-17

Abide in Jesus' Word — you'll know the truth and the truth will make you free (unencumbered by the world)
The Word is profitable for doctrine, reproof, correction, instruction in righteousness (which equips us for good works.)

Matthew 4:19 / Romans 1:16

Follow Jesus to become fishers of men; never ashamed of the gospel of Christ which is the power of God to salvation for everyone who believes.

Luke 11:1 / Philippians 4:6-7

Knows how to pray & teach prayer.
Be anxious for nothing, but in everything by prayer and supplication, with thanksgiving, let your requests be made known to God, and the peace of God, which surpasses all understanding, will guard your hearts & minds thru Christ Jesus.

35

John 14:21 / Luke 6:46

keep commandments - shows love of Jesus - Jesus will manifest Himself to him

Matthew 25:37-40 / Acts 20:35

When did we see you hungry, thirsty, stranger + take in, naked, sick, in prison? Support the weak - more blessed to give than to receive.

16. From these insights, write a two- or three-sentence description of a disciple.

Stay in the word daily, deny yourself, love one another, pray always (ask anything in Jesus' name), keep the commandments, do the word (above). It's more blessed to give than to receive. Be an example for all who see you. Give all these things away to person being mentored.

- How is this second description similar/dissimilar to your first description of a disciple in question #14? *Same*

Review Appendices F and H for additional insight on the description of a disciple.

Alongsiders take action.

17. Why would you want to commit your life to accomplishing the Great Commission? Write a brief paragraph describing your commitment to making disciples.

I recognize ∨that I could be doing so much more to fulfill
from scripture
the great commission than I am presently doing. I need to
grow in my faith & basic tools to become an alongsider.
I am committed to learn what I need to be equipped to
tell others the Good News and reproduce the character of
Jesus in others, as I learn & grow. I want my life to
count for Jesus.

18. Many people have found the practice of forming an alongsider circle to be an effective tool for their discipleship ministry. Read Appendix D and complete the process to develop your alongsider circle.

An alongsider checkup

❏ How would you assess the quality of your appointments with God this past week?
❏ Review Appendices A, B, and C, and try a different approach in your appointments with God this coming week.

John 17 – First 5 verses, Jesus prays for Himself
Rest of John 17 – Jesus' prays for his disciples and following generations! (us)!

CHAPTER FOUR

The Way of Prayer

Alongsiders partner with the Holy Spirit through prayer.

Introduction

When we talk about prayer, it's easy to shift our minds into autopilot. *Here it comes again. Another message on prayer. I've heard this one before,* we think to ourselves. This is unfortunate. Our boredom overwhelms God's invitation to partner with Him in changing the world. God invites us to be His partners in life change through prayer.

We love people when we pray for them. Heartfelt prayer lifts our eyes from ourselves to the needs of others. Prayer teaches us that transformation is a work of God, not of our abilities or techniques. Consistent prayer places our trust in the Holy Spirit and not in our programs. Prayer was the hallmark of Jesus' life and ministry.

Our master disciplemaker began His ministry by spending the night in prayer before selecting twelve men who would be His closest companions (Luke 6:12-13). This commitment to pray continued throughout His ministry (Mark 1:35). Prayer was one of Jesus' most common teaching subjects (Matthew 6:5-13) and is the one spiritual discipline that the disciples asked for instruction in (Luke 11:1). His example of prayer sets the pace for us. As alongsiders, we partner with the Holy Spirit through prayer.

> In the years of active ministry, Jesus changed the moral landscape of the planet. For nearly two thousand years since, he has been using another tactic: prayer. —Philip Yancey

Alongsiders learn from the example of Jesus and the Apostle Paul.

1. From the following passages, what observations can you make about the importance of prayer in Jesus' ministry?

Matthew 14:23   *Went to a mt. alone, to pray in the evening.*

Mark 1:35   *In the morning (early, before daylight) — solitary place*

Luke 6:12   *All night (to the mountain) to God*

John 17:9   *Prays for them ———, not for the world — for those God gave to Jesus.*

John 17:20   *All Jesus' are God's, and God's are Jesus' — Jesus is glorified in (them) — us*

2. Given the demands of Jesus' schedule, what inconveniences or obstacles do you think He had to overcome in order to pray?

Multitudes pressing in on Him
Time
Lack of sleep
Tired

> Talking to men for God is a great thing but talking to God for men is still greater.
> —E. M. Bounds

3. We also face inconveniences or obstacles to prayer. What can we learn from Jesus' life that will help us be faithful in praying for others?

Just do it
Alone
Private, quiet place
Regularly

4. Jesus was an alongsider to Peter, not only in public settings but also in the behind-the-scenes ministry of prayer. Read Luke 22:31-32 and answer the following meditation questions.

- Jesus addressed a future challenge in Peter's life. Read Mark 14:27-31 and describe this challenge. *Satan asked to sift Peter as wheat.*

- What need in Peter's life did Jesus address in prayer?

  That his faith would not fail.

- What does this conversation reveal about the role of spiritual warfare in our lives and the power of prayer to overcome it? *It works, if Jesus did it!*

- What was Jesus' confident expectation regarding the outcome of Peter's testing? Consider John 21:15-19. *He'd win over it, and come back stronger to return to Jesus strengthen his brethren*

- Do you think Peter would have experienced this success if Jesus hadn't prayed?

  probably not.

5. What can you learn from Jesus' example about how to pray for people?

  Intercede, as the Lord brings them to mind.

6. Read John 17:13-19. What did Jesus pray for His disciples? Add to the following list:

- To experience the full measure of Jesus' joy
- Not to be taken from the world
- Protection from the evil one
- _Sends them into the world, even as God sent Jesus_
- _Be sanctified by the truth_

We will never have time for prayer—we must make time. On this score we have to be ruthless with our rationalizations. John Dalrymple rightly observes, "The answer is that we only learn to pray all the time everywhere after we have resolutely set about praying some of the time somewhere."
—Richard Foster

- From John 17:13-19, how would you describe Jesus' motivation for prayer? *Out of love — all for us!*

- Using Jesus' example, what can you pray for regarding the people you're discipling?

  - *Have Jesus' joy fulfilled in themselves*
  - *Keep them from the evil one (Satan).*

7. How would you complete the following sentence? "As an alongsider, I'm motivated to pray because . . ."

   God answers the prayers of the righteous
   Those discipled need encouragement

8. The Apostle Paul was also committed to prayer. What do you learn about his prayer life in Ephesians 1:16 and Colossians 1:9?

   - *Mentions his disciples in prayer*
   - *Thankful for them*
   They Be filled with the knowledge of His will in wisdom & spiritual understanding.

- Consider Paul's prayers for the Ephesian believers in Ephesians 1:15-19 and 3:14-19. From these two prayers, develop a list of all the things that Paul prayed for these men and women.

  1. give thanks for them and circumstances of their lives.
  2. spirit of wisdom + revelation in the knowledge of God.
  3. understanding
     a) hope of his calling
     b) their inheritance
     c) greatness of his power
  e) Strengthened through the Spirit in the inner man
  f) thru faith, Christ dwell in their hearts
  g) understand the love of God, wide, deep, length

- How was spiritual transformation at the heart of Paul's prayer life?

  In everything he prayed!

9. Summarize your findings on prayer in the following chart.

When should I pray?	*at all times (without ceasing)*
Why should I pray?	*— God gives to his children who ask* *— Satan doesn't want us to pray* *— That the saints may grow in knowledge + power*
How should I pray?	*— ACTS* *— as Jesus prayed, with faith.*
What should I pray?	*Anything + everything*

Alongsiders take action.

10. Here are three possible ways to partner with the Holy Spirit in prayer.

- **Create a plan.** Prayer requests can be recorded on 3x5 cards, in a daily planner, or with your smartphone. What personal plan for recording prayer requests will you use?
- **Set aside a time and place.** Praying for people can occur as you commute to work, exercise, or walk the dog. When and where will you pray for people?
- **Regularly solicit prayer requests.** What are the most current prayer concerns of the people you're discipling?

11. Prayerfully think through a practical application using one of the ideas in question #10.

This coming week, I will *list prayer requests in my smartphone.*

An alongsider checkup

❑ How would you assess the quality of your appointments with God this past week?
❑ Whom have you identified to invite into your alongsider circle?

Part Two:

Skills

CHAPTER FIVE

The Way of Relationships

Alongsiders build authentic friendships.

Introduction

So much of life happens in common places—the routines of where we live, work, or play. Eugene Peterson describes how "most [personal ministry] takes place in obscurity: deciphering grace in the shadows."[1] These "shadows" are the everyday events where we comfort a friend, read the Bible with a son or daughter, or lead a small group in a living room. Without fanfare or applause, we build relationships in the common places of life.

The author of Deuteronomy understood the value of the common place. For the nation of Israel to follow God's ways, they needed a vision for planting truth in daily routines:

> It's hard for us to come clean and admit it. We're afraid that if we tell it like it is, we'll ruin our testimony. What we fail to understand is that our refusal to bring to light what we really are, to be honest about our sins, fears, and struggles, leaves us with no testimony at all.
> —Jim Petersen

> You shall love the LORD your God with all your heart and with all your soul and with all your might. These words, which I am commanding you today, shall be on your heart. You shall teach them diligently to your sons and shall talk of them when you sit in your house and when you walk by the way and when you lie down and when you rise up. . . . You shall write them on the doorposts of your house and on your gates. (Deuteronomy 6:5-7,9, NASB)

"It is in the common place," writes Oswald Chambers, "where there is no witness, no limelight, no one paying the remotest attention that God is glorified."[2] Packed auditoriums and successful programs are not prerequisites for Jesus' disciples. God loves to work in the shadows of the kitchen table or the leisurely walk of friends together. This is where relationships are built.

Relationships, whether in large groups, small groups, or one-to-one, are the indispensable element for disciplemaking. However, when we intentionally come alongside people in authentic relationships, our lives soon become transparent. We can't hide our disappointments and joys. Alongsiders are never asked to be perfect, but they are called to be authentic, trusting the Holy Spirit to exhibit love, transparency, and vulnerability to others. This authenticity is found in the here and now of family, neighbors, or church relationships. Alongsiders believe that doing the Great Commission happens one relationship, one conversation, at a time.

Alongsiders learn from Jesus' example.

Jesus built relationships in the common places of life. Most of His ministry took place outside of religious setting. It was in the ordinariness of life, shared with His twelve companions, that our Lord lived authentically, displaying love, transparency, and vulnerability to others. Consider these shared events:

John 2:1-11	Jesus attended a wedding with His disciples.
Matthew 9:10	Jesus and His disciples enjoyed a social dinner at Matthew's home.
Matthew 13:54	Jesus, with His disciples, participated in public worship.
Matthew 19:13	Jesus, with His disciples, enjoyed the presence of children.
Mark 1:29	Jesus and His followers visited a friend's home.
John 11:1-2	Jesus and His followers stayed with friends Martha and Mary.
John 13:2	Jesus shared the Passover meal with His disciples.

1. What does this diverse set of events tell us about how Jesus built relationships with the people He was discipling?

   In ordinary events

   • Why do you think Jesus valued these common places and events?

   1) It made Him real and non-threatening to his friends.
   2) He enjoyed relating to others

2. What are some common places in your life to build relationships? Add to this list.

   • Workplace
   • Neighbors   *opera!?*
   • Small group at church
   • Friends from school or college
   • *Gym*
   • *Cards*

3. Why are relationships, built in common places, so critical to the alongsider? Add to the following observations:

- We see each other as we really are.
- We ask one another important questions.
- We spontaneously and naturally respond to life.
- We discover how informality reveals our true values and beliefs.
- _____
- _____

4. People are busy in the twenty-first century. How can you come alongside these busy people to build friendships? Add to the following list:

- We can eat a meal together.
- We can go shopping together.
- We can pursue a hobby together.
- We can invite one another over to help on a house project.
- We can visit one another's homes.
- *Play cards*
- *Golf*

5. In Mark 3:14, Jesus chose twelve to "be with him." This short phrase embodies a powerful alongsider principle. Author Robert Coleman describes it best:

> He did not ask anyone to do or be anything which first He had not demonstrated in His own life, thereby, not only providing its workability, but also its relevance to His mission in life. . . . It is well enough to tell people what we mean, but it is infinitely better to show them how to do it.[3]

Alongsiders do not give instructions from a distance. They intentionally come alongside people in the classroom of life, demonstrating how to love God and live on mission. Alongsiders don't *tell* people the way of Jesus; they personally *show* others how to live like Jesus. Practicing the "with Him" principle happens when we:

- Have a quiet time with someone rather than telling how to have a quiet time.
- Do Bible study with someone rather than exhorting him or her to study the Bible.
- Invite him or her to see how we relate to our spouses, children, or roommates rather than explaining the value of relationships.

invite over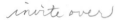

If he would serve God and reach heaven, he must find companions or make them. The Bible knows nothing of solitary religion.
—John Wesley

What other examples of the "with Him" principle could you provide?

- Attend events they're involved with.

- Remember to celebrate birthdays & events with them

Alongsiders value the entire body of Christ.

6. While disciplemaking is often pictured as an individualistic ministry, God intends to engage the entire body of Christ in the disciplemaking process. He deliberately plants each of us in the soil of His body. Read Ephesians 4:11-16 and reflect on the following questions.

   • How should each of us relate to one another?

   Use our talents, edify one another, each does it's share, speak the truth in love. grow in unity

   • How does God uniquely design each of us to bring the body (all of us) to maturity (verses 11-12)?

   He made some apostles, prophets, evangelists, pastors, teachers to equip the saints for the work of ministry.

   • What happens if one part of the body fails to do his or her part?

   The whole body suffers.

7. The Apostle Paul understood the value of each of us contributing to the lives of others. In 1 Thessalonians 3:10, he wrote, "Night and day we pray most earnestly that we may see you again and **supply what is lacking** in your faith" (emphasis added). God uses each of us to supply what's lacking in one another's faith. This is more than a one-way street. In Romans 1:11-12, Paul said, "I long to see you so that I may impart to you some spiritual gift to make you strong—that is, that you and I **may be mutually encouraged** by each other's faith" (emphasis added).

   • If ministry is one-sided, with only one person qualified to minister to another, what could happen?

   One ~~or the other~~ could burn out.

8. Review the network of believers you associate with. What various gifts, strengths, and experiences could they contribute to help you grow in Christ?

Jean – hospitality, encourager   Claudia – helps, prayer
Bobbie – teacher
Sandy – prayer, helps
Carol – organizer

- How can you tap into this network to help the people you're an alongsider to?

  Spend time with them & learn from them.

Alongsiders live authentically with love, transparency, and vulnerability.

9. **Love.** Consider John 13:1: "Having loved his own who were in the world, he now showed the full extent of his love." **Love is both an <u>unconditional acceptance</u> of people and a <u>volitional choice</u> to seek another's highest good.**

- Picture yourself as one of the twelve disciples. How do you think you would have experienced Jesus' love for you as you traveled with Him? *1) Jesus saying "I still love you" when we blow it.*
  2) Mary & Martha – rebuke, but accepted
  3) Pray with me – in Gethsemene.

> To love at all is to be vulnerable. Love anything, and your heart will certainly be wrung and possibly be broken. —C. S. Lewis

Love can be displayed in simple gestures. What are ways that alongsiders can love the people they're discipling? Add to this list:

- I can remember birthdays, anniversaries, and so forth.
- I can spontaneously call, text message, or email to share appreciation and affirmation.
- I can smile and describe how glad I am to see him or her.
- *Hug & smile*
- *Give gifts*

10. **Transparency.** Jesus displayed this wonderful quality in this simple statement: "You are those who have stood by me in my trials" (Luke 22:28). To "stand" with someone is more than observing personal needs from a distance. It means getting up close to personally support in times of need. To be supported by someone else requires expressing the need for help. For the disciples to stand by Jesus in His trials, He first had to share His trials with them (Hebrews 4:15)! **Transparency is a willingness to expose my personal struggles, fears, and life issues inside the safety of a friendship.**

- If you were one of the Twelve, how do you think you would have witnessed Jesus' transparency?

  1) Pray with me in my entreaty of God
  2) Let's go get some food
  3) Let's go visit Mary & Martha

- Transparency can be expressed by making self-revealing statements. For example, you might say, "Today I feel sad and discouraged." What other self-revealing statements could you make?

  I feel vulnerable
  "   "   scared
  "   "   tense
  "   "   overwhelmed

> When we speak of virtues we are competitors; when we confess our sins we become brothers.
> —Karl Barth

- Do you think there are limits to the degree of transparency we should display with others? Explain your answer.

  Some things could be really personal

11. **Vulnerability.** Jesus demonstrated His vulnerability in a variety of ways. Here is one example:

   He took Peter and the two sons of Zebedee along with him, and he began to be sorrowful and troubled. Then he said to them, "My soul is overwhelmed with sorrow to the point of death. Stay here and keep watch with me." (Matthew 26:37-38)

   Vulnerability moves a step beyond transparency. **Vulnerability does more than share needs or hurts. It invites people into my life to help support, encourage, or correct me in times of need.**

- What can you learn about Jesus' vulnerability from His struggle in Gethsemane in Matthew 26?

*Sweat drops of blood
My flesh is scared
Come pray with me.*

We choose to be vulnerable when we ask for help. Asking for help could include the following. Add to these examples:

- I need advice in raising children.
- I want to know how to deal with an irritating coworker.
- I am struggling with loving my spouse.
- *I'm in an unhealthy relationship*
- *I'm depressed*
- *I'm having surgery – scared*

Alongsiders enter the life stories of others.

When we authentically move into another's life, we discover that our lives are like a good story. Good novels absorb us in their plots, characters, and action. Our lives are like this. Major characters mark us in special ways. Multiple story lines compete for attention. The God-theme of our lives jumps off the page.

Everyone has a God-theme woven into his or her life. For some, this faith story is hidden, almost obscured by life. For others, it's the overwhelming plot. Alongsiders know how to skillfully read the God-themes of their neighbors, relatives, or coworkers. When we read the story line of faith, we discover how God is at work. We can then join in and become the Holy Spirit's partner for change. However, as readers, we do not barge into the life of another. We win the right to read another's life. This right is won through authenticity—the demonstration of love, transparency, and vulnerability.

> In evangelical circles so often we try to apply formulas to each other with total disregard for where we are in our own story.
> —John Eldredge

How can you get started in reading the novel of another's life? How can you discover the God-theme that is present? One practical way is to share your faith stories.

In your next alongsider time, ask your friend to come prepared with a timeline of his or her life. On this line, have your friend mark important events, friendships, successes, failures, or lessons that shaped his or her spiritual growth. Do this assignment yourself. Then, over a cup of coffee or a meal, share your story lines with one another. You will soon discover how God has been uniquely at work in the quiet of each other's life.

To get started, list some important events, people, and so forth on the timeline below and briefly note how God used them to shape your faith story. Then set up a time to meet with the person you're an alongsider to and share your stories.

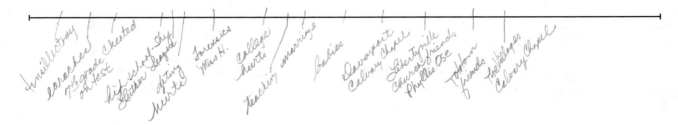

Alongsiders take action.

Has your picture of disciplemaking changed as a result of this chapter? Describe any changes.

Principle	What one discovery or truth stood out to you from this study?
	The need for transparency in building friendships.
Personal	If you believe this truth to be true, how could it impact your life within the next twenty-four hours? Brainstorm several possibilities.
	Closer to Glenn
Practical	What measurable action step could you take to apply this principle within the next twenty-four hours? Describe the what, when, where, and how.
	Talk – sharing examples from the past. Both share specific times

Alongsiders practice VIM.

V	Relationships are essential for discipling others.
I	I will take the time and effort to build quality friendships.
M	I will complete the "Taking Action" section of the study and identify at least one way to show love, transparency, or vulnerability this week.

An alongsider checkup

❏ What new approach from the appendices did you try in your appointments with God this past week?

❏ Whom did you invite into your alongsider circle?

❏ How would you describe your prayer life for those in your alongsider circle?

CHAPTER SIX

The Way of Depth

Alongsiders go deep in relationships.

Introduction

If you could make one phone call in an emergency, who's the friend you would contact? The people we call in emergencies are usually our closest friends. Quality relationships have a depth and closeness that move beyond the superficial to the issues of the soul. Philip Yancey writes, "Relationships deepen as I trust my friends with secrets."[1] Alongsiders know how to go deep with people, creating relationships of trust that give room for the Holy Spirit to work.

Jesus was a master at going deep with people. In the conversations recorded in the Gospels, Jesus dispensed with clichés and quickly moved to issues of the heart. He was never satisfied with the status quo of a person's life. Whether with a tax collector, Roman soldier, or Samaritan woman, Jesus went deep with people, challenging them for life change.

How did He do this? Jesus established common ground, probed with searching questions, and made insightful observations that tapped into the deep longings and hurts of others. Our Lord sensitively started at a person's point of need and moved him or her toward change. Following Jesus' example, alongsiders know how to go deep with people.

We intentionally go deep with people by living authentic lives. With transparency comes great trust. When we live authentically, people give us permission to enter their God-stories. By **listening** and practicing **five levels of communication**, we come alongside the story that God is shaping in people's lives. When a friend invites us into his or her God-story, we've earned the right to be a change agent for Christ. How can we practically do this? The following exercises will show you how.

> No one can develop freely in this world and find a full life without feeling understood by at least one person. No one comes to know himself through introspection. . . . Rather it is dialogue, in his meeting with other persons.
> —Paul Tournier

Alongsiders go deep through listening.

1. What instructions do James 1:19, Proverbs 18:13, and Proverbs 25:12 provide for good listening?

2. The following are some good and bad listening habits. Place an X before the habits that irritate you the most. Place a T before the habits that are true of you (both good and bad).

X__ He/She doesn't give me a chance to talk; I go with a problem and never get a chance to talk about it.

T__ He/She gives me his/her undivided attention when I'm speaking.

X__ He/She interrupts me when I talk.

___ He/She asks questions after listening rather than immediately providing answers.

___ He/She never looks at me when I talk; I don't know if he/she is listening to me.

T__ He/She makes repeated and sensitive eye contact with me when I'm talking.

___ He/She continually fidgets with a pencil, paper, or some other object, looking at it and examining it rather than listening to me.

T__ He/She uses facial expressions to communicate that he/she is listening.

X__ He/She never smiles. I'm afraid to talk to him/her.

___ He/She smiles often, which invites me to talk further.

___ He/She often gets me off the subject with his/her questions or comments.

___ He/She asks questions that encourage me to further explain myself.

X He/She throws cold water on my suggestions, so I've quit making suggestions.

__ He/She often affirms what I'm saying and encourages my conversation.

X He/She is always rushed for time, commenting about his or her busy day.

__ He/She communicates that I have his/her full attention.

- List your strengths and weaknesses when listening.

  eye contact
  smile
  nod – "I'm listening"

- How can active listening affect how deep you go in discipling another?

  Comments are springboards for more questions, more sharing

- What do you listen for in discipling another? Add to the following suggestions:

  ❏ Do I know his or her faith story?
  ❏ What do I know about his or her important relationships, values, and priorities?
  ❏ What do I know about the people and events that have shaped his or her life?
  ❏ How does the person describe his or her relationship with God?
  ❏ Does he or she often complain or does that person describe how he or she is trusting God for the details of life?
  ❏ _____
  ❏ _____

Alongsiders intentionally go deep one step at a time.

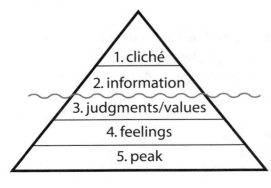

1. cliché
2. information
3. judgments/values
4. feelings
5. peak

Relationships are only as good as the communication between people. When we honestly tell each other who we are—what we think, love, hate, fear, and dream about—then we can begin to grow. This type of authentic friendship is built one step at a time.

When we go deep with people, we're moving into areas that lie below the surface of their lives. Our attitudes and performance can be like the tip of the iceberg, the portion

visible to others. Below this tip is a deeper life—our true motives, values, and attitudes. Alongsiders walk with people in authentic ways so that we can go below the surface in people's lives. This is where Jesus wants to transform us. How do we do this?

Going deep means traveling through five levels of communication.[2] The first two levels represent the least amount of willingness to disclose ourselves; this is the tip of the iceberg. The successive, descending levels take us into areas submerged below the surface of people's lives. These areas are reached through the remaining levels of communication.

▲ Level 1: Cliché conversation

This is the lowest level of communication. In fact, there is no communication at all except by accident. At this level, we talk in clichés: "How are you?" "How's your family?" "How's the day going?"

3. What other clichés do you frequently hear people use?

Are you doing well?
What's happening with ———?

▲ Level 2: Reporting information

In Level Two, we remain content to give out information. We offer no personal commentary on these facts. For example: "My name is Jim and I live on Webster Road" or "I work at Richland Manufacturing."

4. What other types of facts are exchanged at this level?

For Villagers — where are you from?
Do you enjoy golf
What are you involved in? (What keeps you busy?)

▲ Level 3: Ideas, judgments, and values

5. Communication is beginning to blossom at this level. Now I'm willing to risk telling my ideas and revealing some judgments and decisions. We watch each other carefully to gauge a response to these disclosures and decide whether to go deeper. Here are some examples of disclosing ideas and judgments. Add two or three examples of your own.

   • I don't think pop music is as good as it was in the 1960s.
   • I have some hesitancy about voting for this political candidate.

- I could not support that store moving into our community.
- I find Pastor John's sermons to be lacking in imagination.
- I wish my wife would wear that color more often.
- *I like what you're wearing — hair style*
- _____
- _____

◢ Level 4: Feelings and emotions (heart communication)

If we really want to get to know one another, we'll share what is <u>on our hearts</u> as well as <u>in our heads.</u> Feelings lie below our ideas and judgments. When I share my feelings, I tell you who I really am. If I tell you only the contents of my mind, I will be withholding a great deal about myself, especially in those areas where I'm most deeply myself.

Consider these Level Four statements.

- I'm deeply offended by the lyrics in most pop music today.
- I fear that the values of this candidate will destroy our country.
- I think it's a crime how some companies underpay their employees.
- Pastor John puts me to sleep when he preaches.
- My wife is really sexy when she wears that color.

6. How are these different from the Level Three statements?
You're sharing your values and risk being judged, criticized

7. How would you evaluate the Level Four conversations with the people you're discipling?

> Within each human person there is a deep need to be heard as a real person, a person of importance who merits attention and respect.
> —David Augsburger

◢ Level 5: Peak communication

Deep and authentic relationships are based on transparency and vulnerability. Real communication is a point of total empathy and understanding. We're peering into one another's souls and asking God to change us. What characterizes peak communication?

- I honestly admit my failures.
- I ask God and others for help.
- I'm free to share this "gut" response because I know that I won't be judged by my friend.
- We easily slip into peak communication even when we've been absent from one another for some time.
- I feel confident that what I share will be held in confidence.

8. What do you think hinders peak communication?

Lack of trust
Unwillingness to share feelings
Lies
Speaking in generalities – not specific

9. What encourages peak communication?

Transparency on your part.
facial expressions, tears

Alongsiders take action.

10. List each person in your discipleship circle. Which level of communication (1–5) is most characteristic of this relationship? Now indicate your satisfaction with each level with an A (excellent), B (growing), C (just starting), or F (failing).

Friend	Level of Communication	Grade

- Chose one friend and list several action steps you could take to move this relationship to the next level.

- Describe one action step you could take in the next week with this friend.

An alongsider checkup

❏ Which tool did you use to meet with God this past week?
❏ How would you describe your prayer life for those in your alongsider circle?
❏ What did you apply from the study on living authentically?
❏ What did you learn about the people in your alongsider circle when you shared your faith stories?

THE Ways
OF THE
Along sider

The Way of the Word

Alongsiders help others love and live the Scriptures.

Introduction

What would happen if all our disciplemaking resources were to vanish and we had only a Bible? How would our ministries be affected if we couldn't rely on the latest book from Max Lucado or Beth Moore? What if we could use only the Bible? Would we be prepared?

We hold in our hands God's means of transformation, the Bible. This book should be at the center of an alongsider's discipling relationships. While we can profit greatly from study aids, commentaries, and devotional authors, we must not substitute them for a firsthand experience of the Scriptures. Alongsiders love and live the Scriptures.

The way of the Word was Jesus' way. God's Word was embedded in the soul of His life and ministry. The Scriptures were not footnotes to validate what He did but were the source of His life. Jesus lived and loved the Scriptures. He submitted to their authority and drew upon God's Word for strength in a time of need. When we come alongside people in life2life ways, we invite them to live the way of the Word. There should always be an open Bible between me and the person I'm discipling.

> Without personal strategies for connecting with God, our daily agendas tend to become: I must have, I must be, I must achieve. But exercises such as Scripture meditation cultivate the heart and guard it from these stubborn habits.
> —Jan Johnson

Alongsiders learn from the example of Jesus and the Apostle Paul.

1. Read the following passages and describe how they reveal the priority, power, and authority of the Scriptures in Jesus' life and teaching.

   Mark 7:6-8   *He quoted Isaiah*
   Called them hypocrites

You search the scriptures because in them you think you have eternal life — but you are not willing to come to me that you may have life!

John 5:39-40; (6:63) → *The Spirit gives life — the words I speak to you are spirit and life!*

John 17:4,17 *I have glorified you on the earth and finished the work you have given me to do. Sanctify them by your truth; your word is truth!*

2. Summarize your findings by completing this sentence: "The Scriptures were central to Jesus' life and ministry because . . ." *They are truth — nothing can argue against truth & God's Word.*

3. The Apostle Paul lived the way of the Word. Read 2 Timothy 3:16-17. What does Paul teach about the authority of God's Word and its impact upon our lives?

All scripture is given by inspiration of God, and is profitable for doctrine, reproof, correction, & instruction in righteousness), that the man of God may be complete, thoroughly equipped for every good work.

Illustrating the Bible's impact

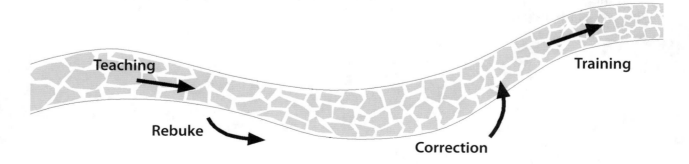

Teaching

Rebuke

Correction

Training

The Scriptures' ministry of **teaching** puts us on the path for living a godly life. We periodically get off the path and need a **rebuke** to show our error. Now the Holy Spirit comes alongside, through the Scriptures, and **corrects us**, showing us how to get back on the path. **Training** is the Bible's ministry to keep us on the path.

4. In Colossians 3:16, we're instructed to admonish and teach one another with the word of Christ. Describe what you think it means to admonish and teach one another. Take time to get to know someone and then sweetly, gently approach the issues at hand

While information about God is important, we need more than this to form an interior, life-transforming relationship with God. What we need is reflection and interaction with God. Scripture meditation proves the opportunity to do this.
—Jan Johnson

- In this passage, we notice the "word of Christ [should] dwell in you richly." What images come to mind when Paul uses the word *dwell*? live there — a house (nice house)

- What do you think a person's life looks like when the word of Christ dwells richly in him or her? Be as specific as possible.
  Able to quote scripture and live it out in daily life. "You know the Bible says",...

5. Why should the word of Christ be at the heart of an alongsider's life and ministry? List two or three reasons.

1. So you are real

2. The word doesn't return void

3. Your life reflects God's image as you practice what you've learned.

Alongsiders have a "grip" on the Scriptures.

One way to illustrate a life where Christ's word dwells in us is through an illustration called the Word Hand. The "hand" shows how to get a grip on the Bible through hearing, reading, studying, memorizing, and meditating.

6. The hand depicts five ways to saturate our lives with the Scriptures. Grade yourself with an A, B, C, D, or F next to each of the following statements. At the end of the assessment, develop an overall grade for your life in the Scriptures.

_C_ I regularly listen to someone who is skilled in teaching the Scriptures.

_D_ I make time on a regular basis to read the Bible.

_D_ I memorize selected portions of the Scriptures.

_C_ I set aside time to ask questions and meditate on the Bible.

_D_ I often make practical applications from what I read or study.

_A_ I'm involved in a small-group Bible study.

_F_ I explore new approaches to meditate on the Scriptures.

_C_ I regularly think about how the Bible applies to my daily life.

_F_ I plan time for personal Bible study into my schedule.

My overall grade: _D_

7. How would you assess your strengths and weaknesses in saturating your life with the Bible?

— No discipline to set up time + schedule

— I'm good at understanding scripture + looking up answers.

• How would you grade the importance of the Bible in the lives of the people you're discipling?

Alongsiders practice truth telling.

In the Scriptures, love and truth are often wrapped in one package. The writer of Proverbs understood this:

> Do not let kindness and truth leave you;
> Bind them around your neck,
> Write them on the tablet of your heart. (Proverbs 3:3, NASB)

The Apostle John described Jesus' life as one lived in this tension of love and truth:

> The Word became flesh, and dwelt among us . . . full of grace and truth. (John 1:14, NASB)

The Apostle Paul described the ministry of love and truth in this way:

> I myself am satisfied about you, my brothers, that you yourselves are full of goodness, filled with all knowledge and able to instruct one another. (Romans 15:14, ESV)

The Apostle Paul encourages us to practice truth-telling in Ephesians 4:15:

> Speaking the truth in love, we are to grow up in every way into him who is the head, into Christ. (ESV)

This sharing of truth happens when we share God's Word with one another:

> Let the word of Christ dwell in you richly, teaching and admonishing one another in all wisdom. (Colossians 3:16, ESV)

8. Why do you think love and truth are so important for our growth in Christ?

   — otherwise you can lose trust
   — without love people will become defensive.

9. What would happen if we had an unhealthy imbalance of only love (showing kindness, goodness, and grace)?

   No change in behavior.

• What would happen if we had an unhealthy imbalance of only telling the truth?

Lose our credibility & respect

10. Describe the marks of a conversation in which we speak the truth in love.

— quietly
— humbly
— respectful

11. Telling the truth focuses on the Scriptures and not our own preferences. How can we tell whether we hold people to a standard of our own preferences rather than the standard of the Scriptures?

Know what the Bible says!

12. What can discourage us from telling the truth in love?

— Not relying on the Word
— not knowing who we are in Christ (lacking confidence)
— fear of rejection

• What can encourage us to tell the truth in love?

— Bible is a 2-edged sword
— know who we are in Christ
— leave it up to H. Spirit to do it His way

Alongsiders help people meditate on the Bible.

The Bible cannot be read like any other book. Casually skimming the words and paragraphs will not transform our lives. Meditation starts by asking the Holy Spirit to help us understand His words: "Open my eyes, that I may behold wondrous things out of your law" (Psalm 119:18, ESV).

Trusting the Holy Spirit, we now dig deeply into the Bible's wealth, slowly savoring God's insights and acting upon our understanding. We do this through meditation, a slow reading process of asking questions and reflecting on our discoveries.

Author Ken Gire describes how the Hebrew word for meditate means "to mutter or to mumble." We mentally go over and over the words, allowing them to penetrate our hearts.[1] Meditation means reading with the head as much as the heart.

Passing on our love for the Scriptures is more than delivering a mini-sermon. Loving and living the Word is a life2life exercise. We spend time with people, in small groups or one-to-one, teaching through the example of meditating on the Bible together. One practical tool to practice meditation is this three-step process:

- **Observation**—taking the first look
- **Investigation**—going deeper
- **Application**—responding in love

Observation. At this point, we're not trying to interpret the Scriptures; we only want to observe closely what's there. Here are some questions to help us take the first look.

- What's going on in this passage?
- Who's talking? Who's listening?
- What are the important words, people, and ideas?
- How do I feel about what's being discussed?

Investigation. Investigation means peering into God's heart as expressed in the passage. These questions will help us go deep to discover new insights:

- What can I discover about God?
- What questions would I like to ask God, or the author, about this passage?
- What can I discover about myself?
- Are there any words or phrases that I need to define?
- What point or main idea is the author communicating?

Application. Application moves the Word from the head to the heart. When we respond in loving application, we're asking the Holy Spirit to change our lives as we obey. Here are some questions to help us respond in love.

- What is one take-away truth to think about today?
- How would I picture God changing my life if I applied this passage?
- What's one specific way I could respond to the Holy Spirit within the next twenty-four hours?

Alongsiders take action.

13. Practice this meditation process using Joshua 1:8.

Observation

We're to always talk about the Scriptures

Investigation

Meditate on God's Word day + night
Be careful to do everything written in it.

Application

Obey and you'll make your way prosperous and have good success!

Alongsiders practice VIM.

V	I want to live and love the Bible.
I	I will choose to meditate more on the Scriptures.
M	I will use the meditation questions from this chapter on two passages this coming week.

During this next week, set aside time to practice this meditation process in two daily appointments with God.

Appointment date and time _____

Appointment date and time _____

An alongsider checkup

❏ How would you assess the quality of your appointments with God this past week?
❏ How would you describe your prayer life for those in your alongsider circle?
❏ What did you discover about the depth of your relationships this past week? Which levels do you primarily act upon?

The Way of Discovery

Alongsiders ask questions, tell stories, and encourage application.

Introduction

Have you ever noticed how hard it is to take down a familiar picture in your home and hang a new one? We become so used to the pictures on our walls that we have no desire to remove them. Comfort, cost, and familiarity keep old pictures hanging in place. In the same way, we have pictures of disciple-making in our minds that are safe, familiar, and sometimes costly to remove. One of these pictures is the picture of teaching.

We have framed the image of the skilled classroom teacher delivering a lecture as an indispensable skill in discipling others. What if Jesus wanted to take down this picture? What would He replace it with? Here's one way to illustrate this new picture.

Two young boys are talking about the dog that sits between them.

"I taught Sadie how to whistle today," says one boy.

The second boy looks at the silent dog and says, "But I don't hear her whistling."

"I said I taught her. I didn't say she learned it," said the first boy.

Sometimes it's easy to divorce learning from teaching. We forget that telling is not teaching and listening is not learning. Teaching is more than delivering a lecture; discovery and application must take place. Alongsiders follow the example of Jesus and encourage learning through discovery.

In the New Testament Greek, the word *disciple* means a learner, someone who follows in the footsteps of a master teacher. Being a pupil of Jesus is something more than sitting in a classroom gathering information or memorizing facts. Disciples embark on a passionate quest to become like their Teacher (Luke 6:40). The Twelve were eager learners, leaving friends, families, and occupations to be Jesus' pupils (Matthew 4:2). Jesus expects the same intensity for learning from His followers today.

> The life of too many Christians—including many in leadership—is best expressed in the epitaph, "Died, age 24. Buried, age 70." Their tombstones will read, "I came, I saw, I concurred."
>
> —Dr. Howard Hendricks

Discovery is the door to real learning. Jesus' students are voracious learners and discoverers. Consider the heart of twentieth-century German pastor and martyr Dietrich Bonhoeffer: "Every day in which I do not penetrate more deeply into the knowledge of God's word in Holy Scripture is a lost day for me."[1] Bonhoeffer was a true disciple.

Learning in the Scriptures is intentional but often informal. While listening to a gifted teacher is important, the Bible also intends for learning to be a life2life experience found in the company of

family and friends (Deuteronomy 6:6-9). All of life is a classroom for Jesus' pupils. Alongsiders purpose-fully open the doors of discovery right where people live, work, and play.

As an alongsider, your task is simple. Instead of an expert who has all the knowledge, you're an intentional partner with a friend in Jesus' classroom of life, life lived in the here and now. Together, you'll make discoveries, explore questions, and encourage application. With the Holy Spirit as your teacher, you purposefully walk arm in arm through life's classroom.

Unfortunately, we can scuttle this voyage of learning and turn it into a conformity of ideas, meth-ods, or curriculums. To encourage life-changing learning, we substitute life for a classroom, questions for lectures, and application for notes. Jesus set the model for us, teaching through discovery.

Alongsiders learn from the example of Jesus.

Ask people on the street what they think of Jesus and they'll probably say, "He was a great teacher." Jesus is pictured as the all-wise lecturer, sitting on a hillside, dispensing truth. This is only half true. Although Jesus preached great messages, He also taught through discovery. His teaching ministry can be placed on a continuum ranging from the formal approach of preaching to the informal approach of discovery. Both were intentionally done to transform lives.

Author Philip Yancey observed that in the Gospels, people approached Jesus with a question 183 times, whereas He replied with a direct answer only three times. "He responded with a different question, a story, or some other indirection. Evidently Jesus wants us to work out answers on our own, using the principles that he taught and lived."[2] The following continuum, from formal to informal, illustrates Jesus' teaching ministry.

Formal Telling					Informal Discovering
Sermon Matthew 5-7	Parable or story Matthew 13	Example John 13:12-17	Assignment Luke 9:1-6	Metaphor John 10:7,11	Questions Mark 12:35-37

If we turn this continuum into a child's playground teeter-totter, most church educational settings would put the weight on the formal end of the teeter-totter, with discovery dangling in the air. Our assumption is that if we've told people something, they've learned it. Information has been transferred, but life is not transformed. Alongsiders help move this teeter-totter up and down, employing the power of discovery.

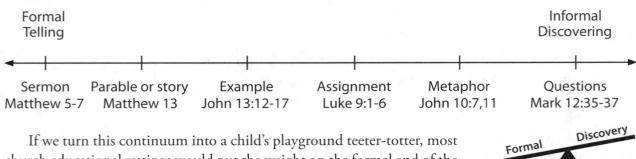

Discovery pulls people from a school classroom to life's classroom. It invites people to move from being spectators to becoming players, leaving the bleachers to play in the learning game.

> The way of discovery happens when we:
> - Ask questions for discovery
> - Illustrate through personal stories
> - Encourage practical application

Alongsiders intentionally ask good questions.

Discovery starts with a good question. Have you ever noticed how God consistently engages His creation through questions? "Where are you?" (Genesis 3:9). "Have you considered my servant Job?" (Job 1:8). "Whom shall I send?" (Isaiah 6:8).

When God asks questions, He's not simply collecting information; after all, He is omniscient. His questions are intended to draw His creation into a relationship in which reflection and discovery take place.

Jesus understood the power of a good question. There are 307 questions recorded in the Gospels. One author described Jesus as "the One who asks questions."[3] A well-placed question acts as an explosion in a conversation, exposing new discoveries, insights, and applications.

Read Mark 12:35-37 and observe this principle in action.

When he finds something that would offer a greater elucidation or apprehension of the story (whether it happens through his own reflection or a divine inspiration in his mind), he will harvest a more delightful taste and more abundant fruit than if the same thing had been extensively narrated and explained by someone else.
—Saint Ignatius

1. What questions did Jesus ask the crowd?

   How is it that the scribes say that the Christ is the Son of David?

- What point do you think He was trying to make?

   Jesus IS - has always been and always will be.

- In this specific case, do you think asking questions was more effective than making statements? Explain your answer.

   People had to think about it more rather than just memorize a fact. sinks in!

Questions to help us L.E.A.R.N.

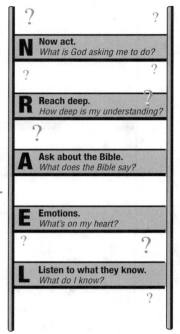

Good questions are like rungs on a ladder. They help us climb from the simple to the more complex. When we apply L.E.A.R.N. questions, we move from discovering what people know to helping them make meaningful applications.

L—Listen to what they know: *What do I know?* Alongsiders want to discover what another person knows about a subject. Learning always begins when someone senses a need for change. Good questions open up holes in our beliefs, creating a need for change. Here are some sample questions:

- How would you describe or define _____?
- What previous experience or training have you received in _____?
- What's your picture of a healthy spiritual life in _____?

E—Emotions: *What's on my heart?* Alongsiders use heart questions to probe emotions and discover motivation. Here are two examples:

- What could light your fire to keep you motivated in _____?
- What disappointments have you faced in _____?

A—Ask about the Bible: *What does the Bible say?* Alongsiders take a person's beliefs and actions and compare them to the Scriptures. Without a biblical picture, we will simply pass on preferences and prejudices. Consider these examples:

- How do you think Jesus modeled _____?
- What examples or principles does the Bible give us for practicing _____?

R—Reach deep: *How deep is my understanding?* Alongsiders go deep by asking questions that help people think deeply and critically about a subject. Shallow thinking produces shallow commitment. Here are some samples:

- What would your life look like if you did not practice _____?
- What do you think you must believe to _____?
- How would you defend your belief in _____?

N—Now act: *What is God asking my to do?* Alongsiders use application questions to turn discoveries into practical action steps. Without application, our discoveries remain pious platitudes, nice thoughts but disconnected from life. Here are two examples:

- How could your life be different in the next twenty-four hours if you applied _____?
- What is one thing you could do in the next twenty-four hours to practice _____?

2. Pause for a moment to assess your question-asking abilities. Which of the following statements describes your view of asking questions?

- ❏ I feel awkward asking questions.
- ❏ I believe you shouldn't ask too many questions because people's lives are private.
- ☒ I often don't know what kinds of questions to ask.
- ❏ I would rather tell someone something than ask a question.
- ❏ I find myself curious about people and enjoy asking questions.
- ☒ I believe that asking good questions is a skill I can learn.

3. What are some ways the Question Ladder can help you in asking questions?

Takes the pressure off me to provide volumes of info.

Alongsiders use personal stories.

Tell a story to people and watch their attention span lengthen. You can see people's eyes sparkle with interest. Why? Stories are about people and places in the here and now—things we get our senses around and automatically identify with. Telling stories, putting principles and ideas into everyday situations, excels as a means of teaching. That's why Jesus was the master storyteller.

Nearly one-fourth of Jesus' recorded words are narratives, true-to-life, could-have-happened stories called parables. Telling short stories was one of Jesus' favorite methods of teaching.

What makes a good story?

> Jesus was a brilliant teacher. He knew how to tell a story that would propel people into thinking in new categories. . . . And he understood the power of a well-timed, well-phrased question.
> —Karen Lee-Thorp

- Good stories **are concise**. Jesus conveyed His points quickly and concisely. For example, the parable of the Good Samaritan is only six verses long with 166 words in English.
- Good stories **connect with the commonplace** events of our lives. Jesus used everyday elements of Palestine: rocks, rain, sand, streams, seeds, fields.
- Good stories **use vivid illustrations**. This means capturing the sights, sounds, and smells of a situation. We can feel the pain of the beaten man in the Good Samaritan parable or the knocking at midnight of the friend seeking bread (Luke 11:5-8).
- Good stories **are personal**. Jesus targeted His stories to the needs and concerns of His listeners. We tell stories around our successes and failures.
- Good stories **help us think**. Jesus often began a story with a question, prodding His listeners to anticipate and consider (Matthew 11:16; Mark 4:30). On other occasions, He introduced a parable with a statement followed with a rhetorical question to prompt listeners to think further: "So you also must be ready. . . . Who then is the faithful and wise servant?" (Matthew 24:44-45).

Each of us has stories, those personal examples that powerfully illustrate vision and character. Our life stories move abstract ideals and hopes into real-life examples.

4. Review the wheel illustration on discipleship (page 115). Identify a life story for one spoke of the wheel. This life story could include some of the following:

- A personal example of succeeding or failing in an area of life.
- A time when God spoke to you through His Word about the importance of this discipleship quality. Be sure to identify the specific verse or passage.
- An example of someone close to you who demonstrated this quality and challenged your life. Make sure it's a first-person story, not one borrowed from a message.

Remember to ask yourself these questions:

1. Is it concise?
2. What everyday experience am I using to connect with someone?
3. Am I using vivid word pictures to capture a mood, sight, sound, or smell?
4. Is it personal, revealing something about myself?
5. How am I provoking someone to think?

Use the space below to begin your story. *Judy Plohn*
Dolores Mann
Mickey
Helen K.

Alongsiders encourage application.

5. Jesus was interested not in transferring information but in encouraging transformation. He expected people to apply what He taught. Consider how Jesus concludes the Sermon on the Mount in Matthew 7:24-27. How does He encourage transformation through obedience?

If you do what I say, this will happen.
If you don't do what I say, your house will fall.

6. Read James 1:22-25. What does James say about the importance of applying (obeying) what we hear?

Will be blessed — otherwise forget (mirror)

Personal application starts with a heartfelt response to the Holy Spirit as He makes the connection from truth to life. It's more than discovery, though. Application takes insight and moves it toward a practical action step. These action steps can be small and silent; no one may see them but the Lord and ourselves. Meaningful applications have three characteristics:

Principle   I respond to a principle or insight from the Scriptures.

Personal   I consider how this principle affects **me**.

Practical   I create a measurable action step to apply the principle. Measurable action steps usually include a what, when, where, and how. For example, simply saying, "I will pray more for my family," is a poor application. A more practical application is "I will pray for my family while I drive to work each morning this coming week."

> Application means to bring together God's truth and God's people in such a way that the people's hearts feel the truth, their minds understand the truth, and their wills act on the truth.
> —Warren Wiersbe

Here are some specific ways to plan an application.

- Can I take a specific **action**?
- Do I need to change my **thinking**?
- Can I make a change in my **relationships**?
- Do I need to make a decision to **study or reflect** more deeply?
- Is God asking me to make a simple response in **prayer**?

Applications are usually an immediate response to the Holy Spirit, something I do today, rather than a long-term action. Applications are simple, daily, and practical responses of obedience to the prompting of the Holy Spirit. They're not usually lifetime decisions or habits.

Alongsiders take action.

Has your picture of disciplemaking changed as a result of this chapter? Describe any changes.

Principle	What one discovery or truth stood out to you from this study?
	Importance of questions
Personal	If you believe this truth to be true, how could it impact your life within the next twenty-four hours? Brainstorm several possibilities.
Practical	What measurable action step could you take to apply this principle within the next twenty-four hours? Describe the what, when, where, and how.

An alongsider checkup

❏ How would you assess the quality of your appointments with God this past week?
❏ How would you describe your prayer life for those in your alongsider circle?
❏ How did you go deep in your alongsider relationships this past week?
❏ Did you teach someone how to meditate on the Word this past week?

The Way of Conversation

Alongsiders initiate purposeful conversations.

Introduction

We live in a culture of change. A walk through any bookstore demonstrates this infatuation. Shelves are stacked with books on how to change our eating, exercise, investments, and social habits. With all this emphasis on change, we must ask ourselves, *Do I place the same emphasis on spiritual change as my culture places on change?*

The Christian life is about change or transformation, a journey to become more like Christ. Author Dallas Willard writes that the "aim [of transformation] is not first to act differently but to become different in our inner being."[1] Becoming different from the inside out was at the heart of Jesus' ministry to His disciples.

Alongsiders journey with people in the process of transformation. We know we haven't arrived, but we intentionally encourage others to join us as we grow in Christ. Alongsiders partner with God and enter into people's God-stories to intentionally encourage transformation. This change process often starts with a **conversation**. In the common places of life, alongsiders purposefully use conversations to encourage others to follow Christ.

> Christian service is not man's attempt to imitate His Lord's life, but an expression of the reality of it within.
> —Jean Fleming

How does the Bible address change? What does it say about conversations? How can we engage people in life-changing conversations? Grab a Bible, a pencil, and a learner's spirit to begin a journey of change and an appreciation of something as simple as a conversation.

Alongsiders believe in change.

1. The Apostle Paul gives a detailed explanation of change in Ephesians 2:1-10. Use the chart on the next page to make some observations about what we've been changed from. Describe what God wants to change us to.

Changed from (Ephesians 2:1-3)	Changed to (Ephesians 2:4-10)
Selfish, rebellious wanderer, trying to find love (sense of belonging) in all the wrong places – sorority, experimenting w/ sex	I wasn't seeking a relationship w/ God/Jesus, but knew what I was doing was wrong. (the Spirit's conviction). Only after I got married and encountered troubles at home (because we were both caught up in selfish behavior) (baggage from the past) that God got a hold of me (us) in His great mercy & love.... grace in His kindness toward us in Christ Jesus.

- Pause for a moment. How was your life once like that of the person in verses 1-3? Be honest and specific.

- How is your life becoming like the description in verses 4-10? Be honest and specific.

2. When we begin our journey with Christ, some transformation happens immediately. Old attitudes, habits, and vices quickly pass away (2 Corinthians 5:17). However, much of our life is a process of transformation. Consider 2 Corinthians 3:18: "And we all, with unveiled face, beholding the glory of the Lord, are being changed into his likeness from one degree of glory to another; for this comes from the Lord who is the Spirit" (RSV). The Greek word for change in this passage is *metamorphoo*, from which we derive our English word *metamorphosis*, meaning a "change in appearance or character."

• What does 2 Corinthians 3:18 teach about change and transformation?

It's an on-going process.

Alongsiders are sensitive to God's timing and His seasons of change.

Timing is everything. The New Testament uses two primary words—*chronos* and *kairos*—to express the Hebrew concept of time. Chronos time is chronological time. It refers to quantity of time or the amount of time passed (Matthew 25:19). Kairos time is about the "right" moment (Mark 1:15) or the moment of opportunity.

> To be fully alive is to pay attention to kairos encounters.
> —Leighton Ford

In teaching, we talk about the "teachable moment," the time when someone is open to learning. This is kairos time, a divine moment of discovery and change. Alongsiders are always on the alert for the kairos moment. We know that God's timetable may be different from our timetable.

Time for the Hebrews was also measured by the rhythms of life. Instead of points on a timeline, the Bible depicts time as a series of constant rhythms:

> Seedtime and harvest,
> cold and heat,
> summer and winter. (Genesis 8:22)

> For everything there is a season, and a time for every matter under heaven:
> a time to be born, and a time to die;
> a time to plant, and a time to pluck up what is planted. (Ecclesiastes 3:1-2, ESV)

The New Testament describes spiritual growth as seasonal rhythms. There's a time to sow and water, plant and harvest (John 4:35-38; 1 Corinthians 3:6-8). For the Jewish mind, life was wrapped up in these rhythms, rhythms that portray life as a journey rather than a timeline.

When we live as alongsiders, we must learn to think in kairos time, spotting the teachable moments, observing the rhythms of the Holy Spirit. We can do this only as we get close enough to people to discern how the Holy Spirit is shaping their life stories.

3. Thinking in biblical time has some significant implications as an alongsider. Add to the following list:

- Alongsiders look for teachable moments in people's lives, knowing they may not be the result of a ministry timetable.
- Alongsiders pray for wisdom. The time for a penetrating question, an appropriate verse, or a hug are not scheduled like appointments in a smartphone.
- Alongsiders don't get discouraged by the moment. If life is a journey, with rhythms of stopping and starting, the final chapter in someone's life is not written yet.
- Alongsiders share what the person needs to hear, not what the alongsider needs to say.
- _____
- _____

Alongsiders intentionally encourage life change, one conversation at a time.

God uses a simple tool to bring about change in our lives. It's the practice of conversation. These every-day events take place in the shadows of our daily routines; they are found in the common places of our lives. Our Lord takes something small, such as an ordinary exchange of words between people, and uses it in a transformative, life2life way.

The Bible is a book of conversations. Beginning with Adam (Genesis 3:8-10) and ending with the Apostle John (Revelation 1:10-12), our Lord engages us in conversation. The Gospels are filled with conversations Jesus had with people. We see Jesus talking with a spiritually eager religious leader (John 3:1-15), an adulterous Samaritan woman (John 4:1-27), and a disappointed disciple (John 21:15-19). Conversations are so obvious that we take them for granted.

4. Pause for a moment. What is a recent conversation that impacted your life? Describe in several one- or two-word phrases what happened in this conversation.

Sanctification of husband — woman forgave me for judging wrongly !?!

Alongsiders are intentional about encouraging change through conversation. We wisely bring all the ways of the alongsider together into conversations marked by love and truth, authenticity and discovery. The illustration on page 89 describes an alongsider conversation.

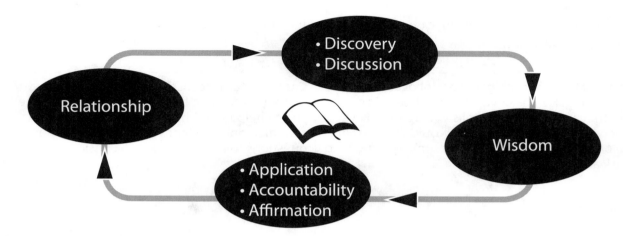

Life-impacting conversations start with authentic **relationships** of love, transparency, and vulnerability. Relationships create safe places for authentic conversations to happen. Alongsiders create conversations around the Scriptures, helping people **discover** truth by asking questions and **discussing** the Word together. Truth-telling naturally takes place as we allow the Scriptures to speak to our hearts and lives. We practice meditation, thinking deeply about the Scriptures.

From discovery and discussion emerges **wisdom**, God-given insight about living in the here and now. Wisdom is then transferred to life with **application**, **accountability**, and **affirmation**. Application encourages practical action steps. Accountability holds others accountable to do what they say. Affirmation supports and encourages us in the process. Without a healthy relationship, application can become legalism, and accountability becomes judgment.

Alongsider conversations can be reactive or proactive. **Reactive** conversations can happen this way. Jane texts you to meet for advice on a relationship. She feels safe talking with you because of the love, vulnerability, and transparency you've shared with one another. Over coffee, you discuss the Scriptures together using the meditation questions on page 71. From these discoveries, God gives wisdom and insight into Jane's concerns.

You naturally ask, "How can the wisdom we've discovered give direction to this relationship?" Application, accountability, and affirmation follow. Through this alongsider conversation, you've helped Jane follow Jesus in the here and now.

Proactive conversations are ones in which you intentionally move a friend toward an agreed-upon picture of a disciple. For example, John wants help in how to share his faith in sensitive ways at work. While eating lunch together, you look at some relevant passages in the Bible on witnessing. Asking questions (using the Question Ladder on page 78) leads to wisdom about what to do.

From these discoveries, you discuss some practical applications. John discovers that he has never learned how to explain the gospel to another. You schedule a future lunch to talk about how to use Romans 6:23 to explain the gospel. An alongsider conversation has just taken place.

The wages of sin is death, but the gift of God is eternal life in Christ Jesus our Lord.

5. Choose one of the following case studies and outline how you would engage someone in an along-sider conversation.

Case #1. Steve can't gain control over his spending. He has never studied the topic of money in the Bible. He calls you up for advice because he trusts you. How would you start an alongsider conversation? List some questions to ask and verses to consider.	**Case #2.** Kathy realizes that she lacks motivation and discipline to read the Bible. She's asked you to help her in this area. How would you start an alongsider conversation? List some questions to ask and verses to consider.

[handwritten in Case #2:]
When are you most alert?
Do you have a quiet space?
What's keeping you from beginning?
Topical? Read Bible in 1-year?
Ask H. Spirit to help you?
Pray about it?

Alongsiders have a pathway for change.

Alongsiders help people along the pathway of evangelism, follow-up, discipling, and equipping. This is not an assembly line to produce disciples but markers pointing the way to fruitful maturity and ministry for Christ.

Everyone travels the path of evangelism, moving from interest to insight to conviction. When we experience **new life** in Christ (2 Corinthians 5:17), we need the essential follow-up elements of love, nourishment, protection, and direction. Follow-up, or spiritual pediatrics (the care of newborns), helps us experience a **growing life** (1 Peter 2:2-3).

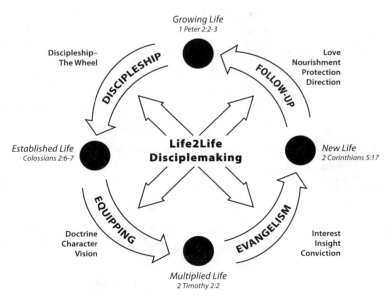

To facilitate growth in our new lives, the Holy Spirit will use the discipleship wheel (page 115) to help us live **established lives** in Christ (Colossians 2:6-7). Discipleship is never an end in itself; we're to multiply our lives as we're equipped in doctrine, character, and vision. The mature disciple is then prepared to **multiply his or her life** (2 Timothy 2:2), reproducing this growth process in another.

What are the important topics to cover in this process? The following chart illustrates some suggested topics for new believers, growing believers, and growing disciples. Remember, God uniquely designs our growth experience. There's no magic formula or how-to manual, but there are markers that point the way. Read through the chart with your alongsider circle in mind.

Who	New believers	Growing believers	Growing disciples
Vision	Growing life →	Established life →	Multiplied life
	2 Corinthians 5:17	Colossians 2:6-7	2 Timothy 2:2
Goal	Get them started	Keep them going	Pass it on
	Initial follow-up of a new believer	Building conviction and consistency	Preparing them to make disciples
Needs	Love, nourishment, protection, direction	Discovery, challenge, application, accountability	Coaching, responsibility, support, experience
Topics	• Reading the Bible • Basic assurances • Wheel illustration • Fellowship	• Daily appointment with God • Cultivating prayer life • Witnessing—personal testimony, loving lost people, starting faith conversations, sharing the gospel • Good works • Serving	• Spiritual disciplines • Basic Bible doctrines • Apologetics • Making disciples • Small-group leadership • Spiritual gifts • Holiness • Faith • Integrity • Stewardship • Bible study skills • Living by priorities
Timetable	one to four months	six to twelve months	one to two years

6. Consider the people in your alongsider circle in light of the chart on page 91. In the appropriate places on the chart, write their names as well as their corresponding needs and topics.

	What is an outstanding growth need?	Review the topics listed on the chart on page 91. Which topics could you cover with him or her?
New believer		
Growing believer		
Growing disciple		

Practical application: Alongsiders work at developing a discipleship tool chest. This tool chest is a collection of practical tools that includes books, small booklets, Bible studies, audio resources, DVDs, and illustrations. A tool chest is a rich source of "means in VIM." Check out the resources found in Appendix G.

Alongsiders take action.

Has your picture of disciplemaking changed as a result of this chapter? Describe any changes.

Principle	What one discovery or truth stood out to you from this study? *Make meaningful conversation*
Personal	If you believe this truth to be true, how could it impact your life within the next twenty-four hours? Brainstorm several possibilities.
Practical	What measurable action step could you take to apply this principle within the next twenty-four hours? Describe the what, when, where, and how.

An alongsider checkup

❑ How would you assess the quality of your appointments with God this past week?
❑ How would you describe your prayer life for those in your alongsider circle?
❑ How did you go deep in your alongsider relationships this past week?
❑ What questions did you use, <u>stories</u> did you tell, or <u>applications</u> did you encourage with someone this past week?   *Mom*   "*I'm sorry*" *to Marge* ⟶ *restoration* "*I forgive you*"

The Way of Mission

Alongsiders recruit people to live as insiders.

Introduction

It was a critical time in Israel's history. Living in captivity, without official representation, Israel faced extermination. Genocide on a massive scale was about to happen (Esther 7:4). The situation was hopeless except for one person on the inside of the king's palace. Her name was Esther and she was an **insider**, someone providentially appointed "for such a time as this" (Esther 4:14). Esther's influence with the king proved to be the turning point that saved Israel from annihilation.

All of us are insiders to work, family, or social settings. While we may not be faced with the momentous opportunity of an Esther, God has providentially placed us in special groups of people to advance the gospel. He has called us to live on mission, entrusting us with the task of evangelism.

Living on mission means hanging the new picture of an insider. An insider shares a common space, purpose, or interest with a group of people. We're all insiders to somewhere and to someone.[1] Whether in the workplace, the PTA, or a fitness club, each of us lives, works, and plays in places uniquely designed by God for the sake of the gospel. Insiders are God's agents for church growth.

Unfortunately, most church growth today is the reshuffling of the same deck of cards. We grow by adding believers from other congregations rather than seeing new conversions. We need simple, relational strategies that go to people where they live, work, or play.

Making disciples is not an end in itself. God's heart beats for the world. When we understand His heart, we're compelled to live on mission for Him (John 17:18) and multiply the number of insiders. If every insider is next to someone, then with enough insiders, we can be next to everyone. The gospel will advance through this ever-expanding network of relationships. This is a vision worth getting out of bed for!

When we embrace the Master's heart, evangelism becomes an integral part of the discipleship process, a process that begins as an insider. Our passion is to prepare and send people on mission as

[handwritten: prayer in family meeting]

> Back when we did these big crusades in football stadiums and arenas, the Holy Spirit was really moving. . . . But today, I sense something different is happening. I see evidence that the Holy Spirit is working in a new way. He's moving through people where they work and through one-on-one relationships to accomplish great things. They are demonstrating God's love to those around them, not just with words, but in deed.
> —Billy Graham

insiders, advancing the gospel right where we live, work, and play. When this happens in our churches, growth will be by conversions, not shuffling. We do the Great Commission one conversation and one relationship at a time.

Insiders are a New Testament strategy.

1. Jesus set the example as an insider. Through His incarnation, He lived, worked, and played among people. *The Message* translates John 1:14 this way: "The Word became flesh and blood, and moved into the neighborhood."

> You're surrounded! You've spent years relating to your family, your community and your situation. Some of your relationships are good, some are bad, but they all have the potential for new meaning now that you're a citizen of the Kingdom of God.
> —Jim Petersen

- What does the example of Jesus teach us about the insider ministry? *Go where the people needing discipling are.*

- How did "moving into the neighborhood" enhance Jesus' ministry? *They all got to know Him and learned to trust Him.*

2. Read Mark 5:18-20. On what mission does Jesus send the formerly demon-possessed man? *Go home & tell your own people how much the Lord has done for you and how He has had mercy on you.*

- What can this instruction tell us about the ministry of an insider? *Start where you are planted.*

3. Matthew, the tax collector, is another insider who followed Jesus. Read Matthew 9:9-12. What does this insider immediately do after declaring his allegiance to Christ? *He got up and followed him.*

- Describe the group of people whom Matthew was an "insider" to.

  tax collectors + sinners + some believers

- How did Matthew's insider relationships open up avenues of ministry for Jesus?

  He came to minister to the sick, not the healthy. He had mercy on them: "I desire mercy, not sacrifice."

4. The woman at the well was an insider to an entire village. Read John 4:39-42. What impact did this insider, a common woman wanting water, have upon her village?

   Many Samaritans from her town believed in Him because of her testimony

5. The Apostle Paul's ministry strategy depended on insiders. He was called to go to the Gentiles—those Greeks, Romans, and Asians who did not share the Jewish culture or heritage (Romans 1:5; Acts 9:15). But when we look at the biblical record, an interesting observation emerges. On his missionary journeys, the Apostle Paul usually started with the Jewish synagogues (Acts 13:5,14; 14:1). How, then, did he evangelize the Gentiles?

> Nowhere in the Bible is the world exhorted to "come to church." But the Church's mandate is clear: she must go to the world.
> —Richard Halverson

   Paul was an "outsider" to the Gentiles, but his ministry in the synagogues brought him into contact with God-fearing Greeks and Romans who were insiders to wider Gentile networks (Acts 13:42-43; 14:1; 17:4). It was among these new converts that Paul established spiritual beachheads, new groups of believers who could reach out to their family and friends.

   The Apostle counted on the continued growth of these spiritual offspring to impact their surrounding areas. Because of these insiders, Paul could refer to an entire area as being evangelized (Acts 13:49-50; Romans 15:19). Insiders were essential to the growth of the early church.

   The structure of the early church naturally built on the ministry of insiders. These early groups of believers met in homes (Romans 16:5; Colossians 4:15). These households were both physical settings and groups of people that included an extended family and household slaves (Acts 16:31-34). Because it was illegal for the early church to own property, the physical home and social networks were ideal meeting and growth places for the gospel.

- Why do you think these interconnected social networks were ideal settings for evangelism?

  They were acquainted w/ each other

• First Thessalonians 1:7-8 describes an insider ministry moving from a Roman city to an entire province. What does this example tell us about the power of insiders? Look up the locations on a map to see the impact of this group of believers.

> One candle lights one candle
> Two candles lights four ...

6. Insiders do some simple things. What are some actions of insiders from the following verses?

Matthew 5:16   good deeds

> Paul, Barnabas, Timothy, Silas, and others who took Christianity to the Roman Empire traveled along social networks that gave them entry to, and credibility within, the Hellenized Jewish communities.
> —Rodney Stark

Mark 5:19   Go home to your own people and tell them how much the Lord has done for you, and how He has had mercy on you.

1 Corinthians 9:22-23
Transparency
Become weak (show vulnerability) with the weak.

1 Thessalonians 4:11-12
Lead a quiet life — mind your own business and work with your hands, so that your daily life may win the respect of outsiders and so that you will not be dependent on anybody.

1 Peter 3:15
In your hearts revere Christ as Lord. Always be prepared to give an answer to everyone who asks you to give the reason for the hope that you have. Do it with gentleness & respect.

7. What have you learned so far about the impact of an insider ministry?

> Meet the needs of the people
> Meet them where they're at
> Be ready to give reason for the hope you have
> Transparency
> Gentleness + respect

8. Visualize yourself as an insider. What are the everyday venues of your life—the places where you live, work, and play? Within these places are people to befriend for Jesus' sake. Using the following illustration, list other social circles of people with whom you're a natural insider.

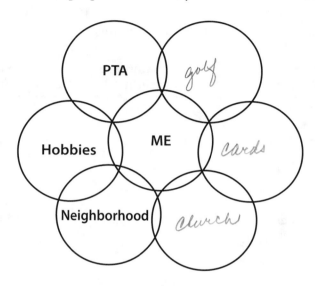

Insiders know that evangelism is a process.

Evangelism is a spiritual process of helping unbelievers respond to the Holy Spirit in a series of mini-decisions that leads them to place their saving faith in Christ. Experience and the Scriptures demonstrate that four things are needed in this process:

- **Relationship**   I'm building relational bridges of trust and respect for the good news.

- **Interest**   My seeking friends are moving from hostility or apathy to curiosity about the Christian faith.

- **Insight**   My friends outside of Christ are making personal discoveries about God, Jesus, the Bible, faith, and so forth.

- **Conviction**   My seeking friends are taking steps to act in faith on their discoveries about God, Jesus, and faith.

The Bible gives us snapshots of people in these four stages. In Matthew 11, we observe how Jesus used social occasions to **build relationships** with lost people. Acts 17 records Paul's conversation with

a Greek audience, people with **interest** but little insight. In John 4, Jesus converses with a woman and leads her to new **insight**. The Ethiopian official in Acts 8 shows how a person responds to **conviction**.

9. Review the friends you listed in question #8. Where would you place each person in the evangelism process? Write their names under the appropriate headings.

Building a Relationship ⟶	Creating Interest ⟶	Leading to Insight ⟶	Encouraging Conviction

10. Read the following practical steps for building relationships, creating interest, leading to insight, and encouraging conviction. Check the steps you could do with a friend listed above.

Building a Relationship
- ❏ I can pray for my friend.
- ❏ I can serve him or her in a practical way.
- ❏ I need to introduce myself to him or her.
- ❏ We can do something together socially: eat lunch together, go to a movie, spend time in my home, attend a sporting event.
- ❏ Other:

Creating Interest
- ❏ I can identify myself as a Christian.
- ❏ I can ask to pray for him or her in a time of crisis or need.
- ❏ I can ask, "Where are you on your spiritual journey?"
- ❏ I can introduce my friend to another Christian friend.
- ❏ I can share a faith story (a simple personal illustration of an answer to prayer, insight from the Scriptures.
- ❏ Other:

Leading to Insight
- ❏ I can share my personal faith story.
- ❏ I can invite him or her to a Bible-reading group.
- ❏ I can invite him or her to a Christmas concert.
- ❏ I can pass on a meaningful book related to an issue of concern or a question we've discussed.
- ❏ Other:

Encouraging Conviction
- ❏ We can discuss his or her objections to the faith over lunch or coffee.
- ❏ We can discuss a gospel illustration (a helpful tool is *One Verse Evangelism* by Randy Raysbrook).
- ❏ We can attend a relevant worship service together.
- ❏ We can talk about what we're learning from a book we're reading together.
- ❏ Other:

11. Which of the practical steps in question #10 can you take to move a current friendship from interest to insight to conviction?

An insider application

12. Review this chapter. What principles or discoveries did you make about insiders or the process of evangelism?

13. Dream a little. What could happen in your small group, adult class, or church if everyone saw themselves as insiders? How could your neighborhood, community, or city be impacted?

14. How do you see yourself living out this principle as an insider where you live, work, and play?

> The conversion of the Roman Empire was accomplished by informal missionaries . . . people chattering [the gospel] to friends and chance acquaintances, in homes and wine shops, on walks and around market stalls.
> —Michael Green

15. Describe one specific action step you could take within the next twenty-four hours to live as an insider for Christ.

Alongsiders do it with VIM.

V	I'm trusting God to build relationships with the three neighbors on my block.
I	I'm going to make myself available to talk with them over the next month.
M	I will invite one neighbor over for dessert or coffee within the next two weeks.

An alongsider checkup

❏ How would you assess the quality of your appointments with God this past week?
❏ How would you describe your prayer life for those in your alongsider circle?
❏ How did you practice the levels of communication this past week?
❏ What did you discover through Bible meditation?
❏ What questions did you use or stories did you tell to encourage someone this past week?
❏ How did you use the evangelism process to identify where people are in your alongsider circle?

What Do I Do Next?

An alongsider action plan

Step 1: Pray.

Prayerfully complete your alongsider circle (see Appendix D).

Step 2: Recruit a triad.

Consider starting a discipleship triad (a group of three) from people in your alongsider circle. A triad has several advantages. It's small enough to:

- Get to know one another
- Easily coordinate schedules
- Encourage application (people can't hide)
- Be successful

Step 3: Choose the Word.

Chose a Bible study that will encourage firsthand investigation and study of the Scriptures. Two resources to consider are the *HighQuest* series (highquest.info) and *A Woman's Journey of Discipleship* (navpress.com).

Step 4: Invite with a vision.

In your invitation, share the vision of the group. "I'm thinking about starting a group of three friends to grow as disciples of Christ. We will meet in a small group for encouragement, study, and accountability. You came to mind as someone who might be interested. Why don't you think about it and I will get back with you."

Step 5: Start with authenticity.

Share your faith stories at the first triad meeting.

Step 6: Ask, don't tell.

This is not a teaching session but a learning experience. Encourage discovery, discussion, and application. Use the Question Ladder to plan questions. Expect completion of assignments and applications.

Step 7: Do it life2life.

Meet with each group member individually every four to six weeks. Start some alongsider conversations.

Step 8: Celebrate wins.

Periodically assess with the group your progress in growing as disciples.

Step 9: Live on mission.

As the friends in the triad are establishing healthy growth patterns, begin to pray about the opportunities to live on mission where they live, work, or play. Help each person identify his or her insider network (pages 99–100).

My Pledge to Be an Alongsider

You've probably never heard of John Baker. Baker had a special passion—collecting and cataloging the films of jazz musicians. John was not a musician; he was a lawyer. He neither played an instrument nor read music. But John Baker was a passionate amateur.

This passion led him to create the world's largest library of jazz performance videos—feature-length productions or small snippets of jazz that would be lost if it weren't for John Baker. His collection is now featured in the American Jazz Museum in Kansas City, Missouri.

Like many amateurs, Baker was obsessed. He became an expert about each of the musicians featured in his collection. Before the Internet came along, he painstakingly tracked down film after film through letters, phone calls, and personal visits. His obsession was not without cost. Every day after work, he would retreat to his den to work on his collection. "That was all he was interested in," said his son. Baker's collection was a bone of contention in the family.

Despite these flaws, John Baker was a magnificent amateur. He did not amass this collection for money but for the joy of the music. In the basement of an ordinary urban home, he meticulously put together a video collection that would become world famous. John Baker loved jazz.[1]

God is looking for ministry amateurs—men and women with a magnificent obsession about loving Him and serving with Him in the Great Commission. Alongsiders make disciples from the sheer joy of knowing Christ. They do this from passion, with excellence, and in the splendor of the ordinary.

Our passion comes from knowing Christ. Because of Him, we invest our energies in the Great Commission (Colossians 1:28-29). Being a ministry amateur is not an excuse for sloppy or half-hearted efforts. We're committed to a life of excellence, "[striving] to excel in building up the church" (1 Corinthians 14:12, RSV). Amateurs take advantage of all the training and experience they can get.

Amateurs work in what Eugene Peterson calls "the splendor of the ordinary." Hidden in a Columbus, Ohio, home, John Baker quietly pursued his hobby. Alongsiders toil in the quiet—the daily routines, conversations, and relationships of everyday life. This is the splendor of the ordinary, the place where God is at work. "As you go, make disciples," said Jesus. Ministry amateurs delight in the splendor of the ordinary.

How about you? Are you ready to make a commitment to be a ministry amateur, an alongsider with a magnificent obsession about making disciples? As you close this journey on the ways of the alongsider, prayerfully consider making one or more of these commitments:

❏ Lord, I want to be an alongsider who is known for my excellence. I will make it a goal to receive further help to be the best ministry amateur I can be.

❏ Lord, I want to get started. I pray that you will provide one person I could disciple this year.

❏ Lord, I'm committed to being intentional. I'm trusting you for a discipleship triad.

❏ Lord, I need the help of others to stay with this magnificent obsession. I will ask _____ to keep me accountable for my action plan.

The 5x5x5 Plan to Read the Bible

How to Experience God Through the Scriptures

The Scriptures are one of God's ordained means for spiritual transformation. The Apostle Paul said it best: "Now I commit you to God and to the word of his grace, which can build you up" (Acts 20:32).

Unfortunately, we can settle for second best in our exposure to the Scriptures. It's easy to read another person's thoughts about the Bible in the latest devotional classic and forfeit a firsthand experience with the Scriptures. It is like kissing someone you love through a pane of glass. There's an illusion of intimacy but little firsthand experience.

The 5x5x5 plan is a simple way to experience God firsthand through the Bible. A 5x5x5 plan is described this way:

 5 minutes a day

If you're not regularly reading the Bible, set a simple goal of reading five minutes a day. Identify a place to begin reading. One of the Gospels or a book such as Philippians is a good place to begin.

 5 days a week

Determine a time and a location to spend your five minutes a day for five days a week. Consider writing this appointment with God on a weekly calendar, in your PDA, or in your daily planner.

 5 ways to approach the Scriptures

We experience God through the Scriptures as we meditate or think about what we read. Meditation helps us go below the surface of the text.

Consider using the following approaches to meditate on the Scriptures during your five minutes of reading. Have a pen and paper available to capture new insights, discoveries, and applications prompted by the Holy Spirit.

Underline or highlight key words and phrases.

Use a pen or highlighter to mark new discoveries from the text. At week's end, review your markings to see what God is teaching you.

Write your own translation.

We write our own translation when we paraphrase, using our own words in a sentence or paragraph.

Ask questions.

Questions unlock new discoveries and meanings. Ask questions using the words *who, what, why, when, where,* and *how.* How would you answer these questions? Jot down your thoughts.

Capture the big idea.

Authors write to communicate key ideas. Periodically ask, "What's the big idea in this verse or passage?"

Personalize the meaning.

When God speaks to us through the Scriptures, we must respond. A helpful habit is personalizing the Bible through application. How would your life be different today if you obeyed what you're reading?

The 5x5x5 is only a suggested plan. You will soon find yourself spending more time in Scripture as God meets you through His Word. Don't become devoted to a plan but to the Person. Record your progress on this thirty-day chart.

30 Days for 5x5x5

You can access the 5x5x5 tool with an attached Bible-reading plan at the Alongsider page at www.navpress.com or www.alongsider.com. Check out other free resources at these websites.

Ten Ways to Recharge Your Daily Appointment with God

1. Try a different perspective. Reading from a different translation gives a different perspective on the Scriptures. It is easy to travel the same well-worn paths in the Bible. An excellent paraphrase is *The Message* by Eugene Peterson.

2. Pray a psalm. The Psalms were originally written as prayers and songs. Read a psalm out loud and voice it as a prayer to God. Use some meditation questions such as these:

- What can I learn about prayer from this psalm?
- What can I learn about God from this prayer?
- What can I learn about how and what to pray from this psalm?

3. Take time to sing. Carry a songbook or a praise CD to sing along with. Many of the traditional hymns are great sources of theology. Spend time praying and reflecting on the words of a hymn or chorus. Sing along with your praise CD.

4. Prime the pump. Priming an old-fashioned pump created the suction to draw the water from the well. We can prime the pump for God by spending five minutes reading a devotional book. *My Utmost For His Highest* (Oswald Chambers), *The Pursuit of God* (A. W. Tozer), or titles by Max Lucado can prime the pump of our hearts to seek God.

5. Get involved. One form of meditation is using all five senses in a historical passage or in the Gospels. Picture yourself standing with Elijah or joining the disciples at the Last Supper. What would you hear, taste, smell, touch, and see?

6. Do it together. Spend time with another person in a daily appointment. Pray together and then discuss the Scriptures. Another person's insights can be a rich source of motivation.

7. Be a reporter. Identify someone in your fellowship or small group who has a vibrant walk with God. Develop three to five questions you could ask that person. These questions could include the following:

- What motivates you to walk with God?
- What do you do in your daily appointments to keep this time fresh?

- How do you discipline yourself to spend daily time with God?
- How has God changed your life as you've spent time with Him?

8. **Learn to journal.** Purchase an inexpensive journal, such as a composition book, and begin recording your thoughts about God, lessons learned, and insights from the Scriptures. I regularly record my insights from the passages I'm studying. This creates my own personal commentary on a book in the Bible.

9. **Paint a picture.** The Bible is full of word-pictures. Illustrate a passage in a picture. Don't worry if they're just stick figures; no one else will see except you and the Father.

10. **Take a hike.** Bodily movement can energize our hearts for God. Walk and pray. As you walk, thank God for the different body parts that are in motion. Praise Him for how He is revealed in the scenery around you.

Putting First Things First

"Putting First Things First" is a simple plan for developing a daily appointment with God. When we place meeting with our Father (the "First") at the top of our schedules, our lives will begin to change. Five simple disciplines can help you plan a time with God.

Discipline #1: Renew. We need to daily renew and refocus our hearts and minds toward God. It's easy to lose perspective. We can renew our hearts and minds by:

- Admitting anxieties and concerns for the day
- Confessing any sin
- Asking God to renew our hearts when we feel tired, bored, or unmotivated
- Reading from a quality devotional guide to set our hearts on God

Discipline #2: Read. The Holy Spirit brings light and life to our lives as we read the Scriptures. When confronted with temptation, Jesus stood on this principle: "Man does not live on bread alone, but on every word that comes from the mouth of God" (Matthew 4:4). Here are some practical suggestions for reading the Bible:

- Decide on a passage to read before you begin your time with God.
- Use a Bible-reading plan.
- Carve out time to stop and reflect.

Discipline #3: Reflect. We must pause to reflect and think about what we've read (Psalm 1:2-3). Meditation is the act of reflecting, investigating, and asking questions about the Scriptures. Here are some questions to help you begin meditating on what you've read in the Bible:

- What did I discover about God?
- What did I discover about myself?
- What did I discover about God's picture of a healthy life?
- Is there a command I need to obey or a sin to avoid?
- What is a "takeaway" thought from this passage that I can continue to think about?

Discipline #4: Respond. We respond in obedience to God through a practical application. Here are some practical ways to think about application:

- Start with a question. *How could my life change if I applied this verse?*
- Make it personal. *How does it apply to me?*
- Keep it practical. *Are there measurable action steps?*

Discipline #5: Record. Some people like to journal and record their insights. Writing down what we're discovering and applying is one more step in the process of remembering and changing. Purchase an inexpensive journal or spiral notebook to record your discoveries and insights as you live in friendship with God.

Alongsiders take action.

- ❏ When will you meet with God this week? _____
- ❏ Where will you spend your appointment with God? _____
- ❏ What passage will you read? _____
- ❏ What things could hinder or distract you from spending time with God? _____
  _____
- ❏ Who will encourage you to spend time with God? _____
- ❏ How many appointments will you aim to keep this week? _____

You can download a free copy of "Putting First Things First" at the Alongsider page at www.navpress.com or www.alongsider.com. Check out other free resources at these websites.

THE **Ways**
OF THE
Alongsider

The Alongsider Circle

An alongsider circle is a helpful place to start in discipling another. This circle is two or three relationships made up of both believers and unbelievers. Here's how to recruit an alongsider circle.

1. Pray. Ask God to provide you with spiritually hungry people who are already on a journey of growth. An example might be an unbelieving neighbor or a friend at work.

2. Think in terms of two or three people. When you complete chapter 10, prayerfully select one person you are an insider with.

3. Review some of the practical ways to build relationships that form a bridge into spiritual conversations. These steps are found on page 99. Select several steps that you will initiate with this person and write them below:

4. Identify some new or growing Christians. Every church congregation has several distinct groups of people. There are new Christians who need immediate follow-up. The second group are growing Christians who want to mature as disciples. A third group are disciples who have heart but lack the vision and know-how to disciple others. Finally, there's the self-satisfied: those who appear satisfied with their current spiritual development and are not interested in additional growth opportunities.

   Who are the new or growing Christians you could invite into your alongsider circle? Work through the following steps to identify one or two people you could invite into an alongsider relationship.

Step 1. God has populated your life with people on a discipleship journey. These people are both inside and outside the walls of your local church. People inside the walls might include:

❏ Small-group members
❏ Sunday school friends
❏ Friends in church ministry teams

❏ House church/home group members
❏ Family members

You have potential disciplemaking opportunities outside the church as well. Are there believers you could recruit to follow Jesus in any of the following categories? Brainstorm and add to this list:

❏ Neighbors
❏ Coworkers
❏ Former classmates from high school or college
❏ Friends from a fitness club, social club, hobby group
❏ Family members
❏ _____
❏ _____

Step 2. Pray and ask God to identify those in whom He is at work. Add specific names to the above categories.

Step 3. Assess the eager and ready people. Here are some signs to look for:

❏ Does this person talk openly about the Lord Jesus?
❏ Is he or she demonstrating a hunger for the Bible?
❏ Is he or she taking small steps of obedience?
❏ Is there a willingness, perhaps awkward, to share their faith with others?
❏ Does he or she discuss answers to prayer or express faith in God?
❏ Is there a genuine regret and repentance over sin?
❏ Does this person discuss the work of the Holy Spirit in his or her life?
❏ Does he or she associate with and befriend other believers?
❏ Is he or she trying to set a Christlike example at home, work, and play?

Step 4. Prayerfully select one or two people and write their names below.

❏ _____
❏ _____

Step 5. Recruit these friends to a discipleship triad (a group of three).

Discipleship as a Wheel

Wheels are helpful metaphors to teach truth. Over the years, The Navigators has used a simple wheel to illustrate the life of a disciple. The following adaptation of the original Navigator wheel illustrates some of the basic qualities of discipleship.

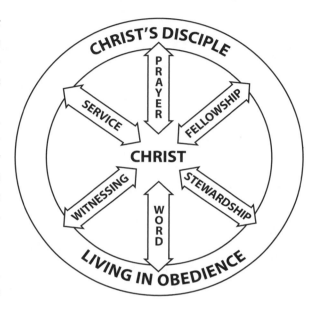

At the center of the wheel is the hub, Jesus Christ. The hub is the driving force behind a wheel's movement. This hub is our **devotion to Christ** (Matthew 22:37). If Jesus is not the Lord of our lives (Luke 9:23), we remain motionless and without life. The vertical spokes illustrate our relationship with God through the disciplines of **prayer** (Philippians 4:6-7) and **the Word** (2 Timothy 3:16-17).

Another spoke represents our involvement with people by **fellowshipping** with believers (Hebrews 10:24-25) and **witnessing** to others (Matthew 4:19). Our **service** to others (Acts 20:35) and the **stewardship** of our time, treasure, and talents are the last spokes (Luke 16:10-12). The rim reminds us that the disciple is in motion, **obeying** the Lord (John 14:21).

When a wheel turns, we do not see the individual spokes, only the hub. It's the same in a disciple's life. Our goal is for the Holy Spirit to transform our lives into Christ's likeness so that He is preeminent in our lives (Galatians 2:20). These disciplines are like the spokes of a wheel, keeping the tension between movement and structure. But a word of caution is needed.

It's easy to confuse means and ends. Perfecting the disciplines, improving one's prayer life, or becoming a more effective witness is not the end. The end is knowing Christ. Our means to get there is the practice of the disciplines. Our goal is not to perfect the means but to get to know the Master!

To add further definition to this wheel, read Appendix F.

The Alongsider Bull's-Eye

How do you spot a disciple in a crowd? Here are some practical goals to build into the life of a disciple.

Characteristic	Demonstration
Matthew 22:37 / Philippians 3:8 A disciple loves God with all of his or her heart.	❏ Practices a daily appointment with God. ❏ Talks about his or her love for God. ❏ Has established two or three motivational reasons for walking with God. ❏ Practices two or three practical disciplines for strengthening a walk with God.
John 13:34-35 / Hebrews 10:24-25 A disciple loves other believers and contributes to another's growth.	❏ Makes it a priority to participate in fellowship activities with other believers. ❏ Does acts of kindness for others. ❏ Is learning to be "others-centered" by putting others' interests above own in conversations or social events.
John 8:31-32 / 2 Timothy 3:16-17 A disciple is committed to living and loving the Scriptures.	❏ Participates in regular Bible study and reading. ❏ Makes regular application of the Bible to his or her life. ❏ Chooses to solve life problems with the Bible. ❏ Expresses his or her love for the Bible.
Luke 9:23 / Galatians 2:20 A disciple is learning to surrender his or her life to Jesus' lordship.	❏ Makes tough decisions to put Christ first in how he or she uses time. ❏ Is beginning to ask, *What would Jesus want me to do in this situation?* ❏ Expresses how he or she is putting God's interests first.

Matthew 4:19 / Romans 1:16
A disciple is growing in his or her heart and ability to share the good news of Jesus with others.

❏ Has identified with Christ to his or her friends or family.
❏ Is learning how to initiate spiritual conversations.
❏ Is able to share personal testimony in a friendly, relevant, and brief manner.
❏ Continues to cultivate unbelieving friends.
❏ Is able to share the gospel with a simple illustration.

Luke 11:1 / Philippians 4:6-7
A disciple is growing in faith as he or she prays.

❏ Shares answers to prayer.
❏ Practices the ACTS principles on a regular basis: Adoration, Confession, Thanksgiving, Supplication.
❏ Expresses how he or she is trusting God through prayer.

John 14:21 / Luke 6:46
A disciple seeks to obey Jesus in the routines of life.

❏ Makes practical applications from the Scriptures.
❏ Describes how he or she is choosing obedience over self-interest.

Matthew 25:37-40 / Acts 20:35
A disciple seeks to serve others through a wise stewardship of his or her time, talents, and treasure.

❏ Is beginning to give to others from his or her income.
❏ Makes self available to serve others.
❏ Has a basic understanding of his or her spiritual gifts.

Planning a Discipleship Curriculum

How can you implement the Discipleship Pathway in a local church?

There are many packaged discipleship curriculums on the market. Here are three examples: *Top Gun* ministry for men (www .topgunministries.org), The Navigators' *2:7 Program* (www.navpress.com), and *A Woman's Journey of Discipleship* (www .navpress.com).

InterVarsity Press (www.gospelcom .net/ivpress) and Zondervan Press (www .zondervan.com) have excellent resources for small-group and personal-discipleship study materials. The following is a list of resources to customize a program for a local church.

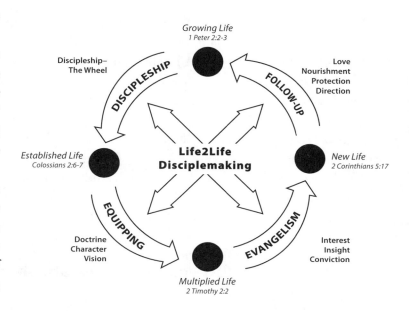

Evangelism—Resources to Move People from Interest to Insight to Conviction

Bible-reading groups invite seekers to read the Scriptures in a discussion format. Consider *Opening the Door* by Ron Bennett (www.navpress.com) or *A Quick Start for Small Group Evangelism* (www .alongsider.com).

Alpha Course—Popular tool to acquaint people with the basics of Christianity (www.alphana.org).

Follow-Up—Resources to Help Growing Christians

Lessons on Assurance—Bite-size studies on the assurance of salvation, forgiveness, prayer, help in temptation, and guidance (www.navpress.com).

7 Minutes with God—Introduction to planning a daily appointment with God (www.navpress.com).

5x5x5 Bible Reading Plan—Go to the Alonsider page at www.navpress.com or www.alongsider.com.

Discipleship—Resources to Help Growing Christians Become Established Christians (Disciples)

Making Friends for Heaven's Sake—A seven-week study guide for small groups that provides practical help in moving acquaintances to spiritual friends (www.alongsider.com).

My Heart—Christ's Home—A booklet on turning all of life over to Christ's lordship (www.gospelcom .net/ivpress).

The Tyranny of the Urgent—A booklet on setting priorities (www.gospelcom.net/ivpress).

Character of a Disciple—*Design for Discipleship* series (www.navpress.com).

How to Have a Quiet Time—Practical resource on deepening the quiet time discipline (www.navpress .com).

The Navigators' 2:7 Series—A three-book study on being a disciple (www.navpress.com).

Thirty Discipleship Exercises—Billy Graham Association (www.BillyGraham.org).

HighQuest—A discipleship program for men and women (www.highquest.info).

Equipping—Resources to Help Established Christians Become Multiplying Christians

Networking—Willow Creek Church's tool for identifying spiritual gifts to serve within the body of Christ (www.willowcreek.com).

Crown Financial Study—An intensive study about God's perspective on finances in the Scriptures (www.crown.org).

The Contagious Christian—DVD, book, and workbook on the essentials of sharing one's faith in Christ (www.zondervan.com).

Living Proof—DVD series and workbook on lifestyle evangelism, published by Christian Business Men's Ministry (www.cbmc.com).

Foundations for Faith (*Design for Discipleship* series)—A study of basic Bible doctrines (www .navpress.com).

The Ways of the Alongsider—A coaching manual on discipling people life2life (www.navpress.com).

Building Blocks for Forming a Disciplemaking Culture in a Local Church

The Ways of the Alongsider is not about developing a program; it is a way of life that's embedded in a church culture. Culture can be defined as a shared set of beliefs, values, and priorities. When someone steps into the life of a congregation, he or she will notice that disciplemaking is a deeply shared value that is preached from the pulpit, modeled in small groups, and transferred in life2life relationships. It is not a measurement of activities or the institution of a program but a long-term effort to build a culture. How do you build this culture of disciplemaking? A disciplemaking culture is like a steam-driven locomotive.

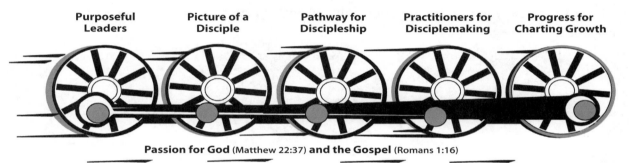

| Purposeful Leaders | Picture of a Disciple | Pathway for Discipleship | Practitioners for Disciplemaking | Progress for Charting Growth |

Passion for God (Matthew 22:37) **and the Gospel** (Romans 1:16)

Steam-driven trains dominate any good western. We immediately picture them roaring down a track, belching out steam, and sounding their whistle. The driveshaft of the train turns the train's wheels and powerfully propels it forward. A disciplemaking culture in a local church is compared to the propulsion of a train. The driveshaft is a **passion** for loving God and sharing the gospel. Without this drive, the wheels will not turn.

The first wheel describes **purposeful** leadership. Without leaders intent on modeling disciplemaking, the culture stays unchanged. Purposeful leaders communicate a shared vision and passion for disciplemaking. What is the disciplemaking vision of your church's leadership? The second wheel is a shared **picture** of a New Testament disciple. This picture is the "target" of a church. When a congregation speaks of discipleship, this mental picture comes to mind. Does your congregation or ministry have a picture of a New Testament disciple?

A strategy for culture change needs more than a picture; it needs a **pathway** to turn the vision into a reality. Here's a way to describe the need of a pathway. When someone walks through the doors of your church and says, "I want to grow as a disciple. How can your church help me?" how will you

answer him or her? A disciplemaking pathway is an integration of large groups, small groups, and life2life ministry. It weaves together biblical content, practical skills, and values that make up the picture of a disciple. How would you answer the inquiry about how the church can help someone become a disciple? Do you have an intentional pathway?

Up to this point, your plan can look good on paper. We have vision from leadership, a biblical picture of a disciple, and a plan to move people forward. Something is still missing. Jesus said, "The harvest is plentiful, but the laborers are few" (Matthew 9:37, ESV). We need **practitioners**, alongsiders who are trained to make disciples. What is your plan for growing and mutiplying alongsiders?

Finally, the fifth wheel describes our **progress**. The book of Acts describes how the "disciples were increasing in number" (6:1, ESV). If a disciplemaking culture is present, then disciples will be multiplied. We will see progress each year in the number of disciples. Are more disciples present in your congregation now than a year ago?

A simple assessment tool for your small group or congregation for building a disciplemaking culture can be found in the free resources at www.alongsider.com. The Church Discipleship Ministry of The Navigators can help you craft an intentional disciplemaking strategy. You can contact CDM at www .navigators.org/cdm.

The Ways
OF THE
Along-sider

How to Turn a Small Group into a Discipleship Group

Step 1: Start over.
It's hard to change the existing culture and traditions of an established group. If you want to become more intentional about discipleship in a small group, disband this group and start over with a new purpose.

Step 2: Invite some new people.
The quickest way to infuse new life and direction into a group is to invite new people. Prayerfully consider who could join this group.

Step 3: Don't fear smallness.
Your new group may be a triad (review the nine steps for becoming an alongsider).

Step 4: Establish VIM.
Describe in the invitation that this is a discipleship group and not a social event or casual group discussion. Intentionality is expressed in a commitment to attend and in personal preparation. The means growth is in every personal preparation, not in a forum for someone to teach.

Step 5: Practice the basics.
A discipleship group is expressed in the basic elements of R + 2D + 3A. We are friends in <u>r</u>elationship with one another who meet for <u>d</u>iscovery and <u>d</u>iscussion, and keep one another <u>a</u>ccountable for <u>a</u>pplications as we seek to <u>a</u>ffirm our growth.

Step 6: Expect preparation.
Choose material that will encourage firsthand study and reflection on the Bible. People will be expected to attend and have their assignments completed.

Step 7: Establish a routine.
Routines build expectations. A simple routine includes a time to pray for others, a time for discussing discoveries, and a time to review applications.

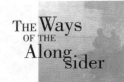

Step 8: Time and consistency build chemistry and commitment.

Establish a time to meet, and maintain this time. Expect people to attend. As you share your lives together, you will build chemistry, which encourages commitment. People will attend because this is where their friends are.

Step 9: Always be on mission.

Periodically evaluate how to add to or multiply your group. The vision is for more groups of friends meeting to encourage discipleship. To start an alongsider ministry in your church, download a free copy of "A Quick Start for Using The Ways of the Alongsider" at the Alongsider page at www.navpress .com or www.alongsider.com.

LEADER'S GUIDE

THE Ways OF THE Alongsider

Contents

Introduction

At our first high school parent-teacher's meeting, the teacher made an observation about my son Ryan. "You know, Bill, not only does Ryan look like you but he has your same speech patterns and gestures. In fact, he even walks like you."

Ryan had subconsciously copied my ways of speaking, gesturing, and walking. There was a "way" about Ryan that reflected me to his teacher. Because we are Jesus' disciples, our lives should remind people of our Lord. There is a way about us that points to Jesus. The Apostles lived this way. Their religious adversaries had to grudgingly admit that "they had been with Jesus" (Acts 4:13, ESV). Their lives were marked by Jesus' ways.

In this Leader's Guide, you will discover ten ways that reflect how Jesus discipled others and learn how to disciple people using the same model He followed.

Welcome to the alongsider adventure.

This Leader's Guide is designed to help you successfully lead a small group using *The Ways of the Alongsider*. The adventure you are beginning is more than reading a book, attending a class, or mastering some skills. The alongsider adventure is all about a lifestyle—helping people minister as alongsiders where they live, work, and play. As a leader, how can you encourage this type of change? Think of it as weather forecasting.

Weather forecasters know that to predict the weather—rain, snow, sunshine, hail—certain conditions must be present. When cold fronts intersect with warm fronts, weather happens. However, there's no guarantee that snow or rain will occur. Certain conditions create the possibility but do not guarantee probability. Spiritual change is like this.

God wonderfully mixes certain elements together to create a climate for change. These are not a guarantee, but they encourage the possibility. For people to begin to live the ways of the alongsider through a small-group experience, these conditions should be present: **R + 2D + 3A**. When you incorporate these elements into your small-group experience, you increase the probability for change.

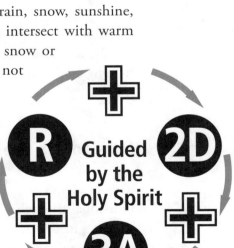

R stands for relationships. As a discussion leader for *The Ways of the Alongsider*, you are not an expert but a guide in the disciplemaking process. Leading people through this material is maximized by doing it one-on-one or in a small group where relationships of trust and accountability can be developed.

2D is for discovery and discussion. Each chapter in *The Ways of the Alongsider* is designed for personal discovery, not as lecture notes for a classroom. It is expected

that the participants will complete each of the chapter assignments. Discoveries are shared in discussion with others. Without the exchange of insights and questions, it's easy to settle for a monologue, thwarting true change.

3A describes application, accountability, and affirmation. *The Ways of the Alongsider* is an application journey. Without application, there is no blessing or change (James 1:22-25). Participants need to apply their discoveries to someone they're an alongsider to. Accountable relationships of trust encourage follow-through and faithfulness to one's application. Affirmation gives an "atta boy!" encouraging people to keep going.

The adventure happens as we learn by doing.

When my six-foot-five eighth-grade son walked into school, the basketball coach started to salivate. Mr. Smith began to picture a conference title. How do you coach someone for success? Mr. Smith could have given Jason an armful of basketball videos accompanied by his stimulating lecture notes. Instead, he played basketball with Jason. He knew that the game could not be learned in a classroom but in the rough and tumble of the court. Mr. Smith's wisdom illustrated a simple principle: **People learn by doing.**

The Ways of the Alongsider is built on this principle of learning by doing. At the conclusion of the book, people will design an action plan to put these principles into action. Along the way, they will practice these principles in the safe setting of a small group or one-to-one relationship. The faith goal of each participant in studying *The Ways of the Alongsider* is the formation of a discipleship triad (a group of three) who are intentionally meeting to grow as disciples of Christ.

Prayer alert! Begin praying now that each person in your small group would be used by God in recruiting and leading a discipleship triad. Watch God multiply your life.

How to use the Leader's Guide.

This Leader's Guide is designed to help you effectively lead a group or work with an individual through *The Ways of the Alongsider*. The Leader's Guide expands the ten chapters in *The Ways of the Alongsider* into twelve sessions. In this Leader's Guide, you will receive a lesson plan for each of the twelve sessions. Each lesson plan includes:

- **Learning goals.** These goals identify what is most important in each chapter. The goals are primarily for the leader and do not have to be shared with the group.

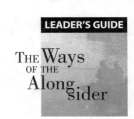

- **Review.** Each week, you will review the previous assignments with the group to encourage application and accountability.

- **Discussion.** Important questions have been identified to help you lead the discussion. Most of the questions are keyed to questions and assignments in the book. Where it's appropriate, the pages and question numbers are provided. **Don't feel obligated to ask each question.** Pick and choose the important questions.

- **Practice.** In each session, people will learn by doing through a practical assignment.

- **Application.** Each person is encouraged to make one specific application.

- **Leader's Review.** Helpful hints are provided to stimulate quality leadership.

- **Notes.** Space is provided for the leader to makes notes to himself or herself.

Four steps to get started.

Step 1. Pray and invite people to study *The Ways of the Alongsider* with you. This is a twelve-week commitment. Each meeting will last about ninety minutes.

Step 2. Have each person purchase a copy of *The Ways of the Alongsider*. Explain that personal preparation is required for each session. You can order copies at www.navpress.com.

Step 3. Set a time and place to discuss the material.

Step 4. As the leader, print a lesson plan for each session and use it as a guide for your time together.

SESSION ONE
The Way of the Amateur

✔ Learning Goals
1. Introduce concepts of alongsider ministry and life2life.
2. Assess people's commitment and skill in making disciples.

✔ Review
Ask each participant:
- Why did you choose to join this group to study *The Ways of the Alongsider*?
- What do you hope to gain by this experience?

✔ Discussion
Select the questions you want to discuss:
- How do you feel about the concept of a ministry amateur?
- How can being an amateur free you to disciple others?
- What pictures hang in your mind about making disciples?
- What is your response to the idea of an "alongsider"?
- How do you feel about becoming an alongsider to someone?
- How is life2life ministry a different picture from other ministry approaches?
- Who has ministered to you in life2life ways?
- Why do you think disciplemaking is so important for church growth?
- What mental pictures will you need to remove to be an alongsider?
- Consider the description of an alongsider on page 15. Do you see yourself making disciples in this way?

✔ Practice
Complete the assessment on page 19.
- What strengths did you discover?
- What are some areas of growth for yourself?

✔ Application
- What is one area you would like to grow in as an alongsider making disciples?

✔ Leader's Review
- If meeting as a group, make sure everyone knows each person's name.
- Affirm each person's contribution.
- Take time to ask clarifying questions during the discussion. "What did you mean by _____?" or "Give me an example of _____" can enrich the conversation.
- Did each person clearly identify one goal from the assessment process?

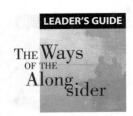

SESSION TWO

The Way of Life

✔ Learning Goals

1. Clarify the biblical concept of being a friend of God.
2. Establish relationship between a close walk with God and fruitfulness in ministry.
3. Practice one tool in having an appointment with God.

✔ Discussion

Select the questions you want to discuss:

- What sustains your heart and hunger for God?
- How would you describe a friend of God?
- Discuss how people answered questions #5 and #6.
- What did you discover about being a friend of God (#7–9)?
- How do you feel about God's invitation of friendship?
- What are the qualities of a friend of God (#12)?
- Why do you want to be a friend of God (#13)?
- Why is spending time with the Father so important in building this friendship (#14)?
- Why is friendship with God so essential to living as an alongsider and making disciples?
- What hindrances do you face in growing as a friend of God?

✔ Practice

Review together the resources in Appendices A, B, and C. Select one of the resources, such as "Putting First Things First," and have a time with God together using this material as a guide. You can download a free copy of "Putting First Things First" at the Alongsider page at www.navpress.com or www.alongsider.com.

✔ Application

Review the "Alongsiders Take Action" assignment on page 28. Discuss the applications.

✔ Leader's Review

- For some, the practices found in Appendices A, B, and C may be elementary. Encourage people that their familiarity with these approaches will help someone else get started.
- Assess your leadership of the group.

  ❏ Did I focus on what is important?
  ❏ Did I encourage participation?
  ❏ Did I affirm people?

❏ Did I make the Bible central to our discussion?
❏ Did we practice learning by doing?
❏ Did I encourage everyone to make an application?

SESSION THREE, PART 1

The Way of Intentionality

✔ Learning Goals

1. Grow in understanding of the Great Commission.
2. Introduce the concept of generations.
3. Describe a disciple.

✔ Review

- Review each person's action step from page 36.
- How did this discipline enrich your time with God?
- Review Appendices A, B, and C and select one practical approach to try this coming week.

✔ Discussion

Select the questions you want to discuss:

- What's your reaction to the idea "Alongsiders think big but start small"?
- Do you think your church has this vision?
- What did you learn about Jesus' intentionality in making disciples (questions #1–5)?
- Read Matthew 28:16-20. From this study, what discoveries did you make about what we call the Great Commission?
- If we turned the "Go" in Matthew 28:18 to "As you go," how could that change how we think about doing the Great Commission?
- Discuss answers to questions #8–9.
- What fears or concerns do you have about making disciples?
- What do you think about the idea of generations? Is this a new or old concept for you?
- Who were the generations that invested in your life?
- Do you think every believer is automatically a disciple? Why or why not?

✔ Application

Discuss together:

- What one truth stood out to you from this discussion?
- How could you apply this truth in the next twenty-four hours?
- Read Appendix D (pages 113–114) for our next session.
- Next time come prepared to discuss questions #15 and #18.

✔ Leader's Review

- How would you describe the group's understanding of making disciples?
- Do you need to clarify or explore anything in the next session to increase understanding?

The Way of Intentionality

✔ Learning Goals
1. Describe a disciple.
2. Describe personal commitment to disciplemaking.
3. Begin the process of recruiting an alongsider circle (triad).

✔ Review
- How did the application from Appendices A, B, and C enrich your walk with God?

✔ Practice
Your group assignment is to take your findings from question #15 (verses on a disciple) and create a picture of a disciple on a large piece of paper. Get started by discussing the essential qualities of a disciple from the Scriptures. Identify these key qualities together. Next brainstorm on the best way to illustrate these qualities.
- How can this picture help us be intentional about discipling others?
- How could our church be helped if we shared a common picture of a disciple?
- Did your original definition of a disciple change from your answer to #14? How did it change?

✔ Application
- Have each person share the paragraph describing their commitment to the Great Commission (#17).
- Ask, "What concerns do you have about recruiting an alongsider circle?"
- Review Appendix D. As a group, walk through steps 1–4.
- Choosing the right person to invest in is an important decision. Be on the alert for God-hungry people. The checklist on page 114 lists characteristics of someone eager to grow. Review the list with the group.

✔ Leader's Review
- Over the next few weeks, pray with them for two people they can come alongside of and invite to a discipleship triad (group of three). The last session will be a discussion of the action plan on pages 103–104.

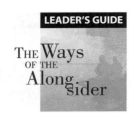

SESSION FOUR
The Way of Prayer

✔ Learning Goals

1. Enhance motivation for prayer.
2. Discover "macro" pictures of prayer from examples of Jesus and Paul. Macro prayers are the big themes of knowing God and character growth.
3. Practically apply principles of prayer in their alongsider ministry.

✔ Review

Discuss "An Alongsider Checkup" on page 44.

✔ Discussion

Select the questions you want to discuss:

- What did you learn from the example of Jesus' prayer life (questions #1–3)?
- Jesus prayed both offensively (Peter's success) and defensively (his protection) in Luke 22:31-32. How can our Lord's example shape how we pray for others?
- From studying an example of Jesus praying (John 17) and Paul's prayers (Ephesians 1), what did you discover about what to pray for in discipling another?
- How can the prayers of Jesus and Paul inform and shape your prayer life?
- Jesus and Paul focused on the big picture of the Christian life. What can you discover about the big picture of prayer (macro prayer) from their prayer examples?
- What are some typical "micro" prayers of people? (hint: finances and health)
- Why is macro prayer so important to the prayer life of an alongsider?
- Review the summary box (#9) on page 43.

✔ Practice

Set aside time during the discussion group to pray some of the "macro" prayers listed in #6 and #8 for each other.

✔ Application

- Discuss how they will partner with the Holy Spirit in prayer from #10–11. Have each person identify one specific action step.
- Spend time praying together for the potential people in each alongsider circle.

✔ Leader's Review

- How can you encourage a spirit of prayer in this group?

The Way of Relationships

✔ Learning Goals
1. Establish biblical importance of relationships.
2. Distinguish between vulnerability and transparency.
3. Encourage one practical application of authenticity.

✔ Review
Discuss "An Alongsider Checkup" on page 55.

✔ Discussion
Select the questions you want to discuss:
- We often place disciplemaking in a classroom. Why do you think Jesus chose "common places" to disciple people?
- How did Jesus establish relationships in the common places (discuss questions #1–2)?
- Why are relationships, built in common places, so important to an alongsider (#3)?
- In today's busy life, how can you come alongside people to build friendships (#4)?
- What did you discover about the "with Him" principle?
- What would disciplemaking look like as we apply the "with Him" principle?
- How can the entire body of Christ be engaged in discipling others (#6–7)?
- How would you describe the quality of "authenticity"?
- Why do you think this is so important?
- Love is a mark of authenticity. Discuss findings from #9.
- What did you discover about the difference between transparency and vulnerability?
- What did you discover about transparency from #10?
- What did you discover about vulnerability from #11?
- If you're not practicing authenticity with people, how will your ministry as an alongsider be affected?

✔ Practice
Encourage authenticity by having people share their timelines from the assignment on page 54. Have each person come ready to share his or her timeline at the next session.

✔ Application
Ask the group, "What is one discovery or affirmation from this session?" Follow up with this question: "What could happen in your life if you applied this discovery within the next twenty-four hours?"

✔ Leader's Review

- Authenticity starts with the leader. What is one way you can model vulnerability and transparency?

SESSION SIX
The Way of Depth

✔ Learning Goals
1. Identify strengths and weaknesses in listening.
2. Discover the five levels of communication.

✔ Review
Discuss "An Alongsider Checkup" on page 63. Have one or two people briefly share their timelines with the group.

✔ Discussion
Select the questions you want to discuss:
- How would you describe your ability to go deep with people?
- How do you know when a depth of relationship has occurred?
- Why do you think it can be scary for some to go deep in relationships?
- What did you discover about your good and bad listening habits?
- Why is listening so important in going deep with people?
- What do you listen for in discipling another? Discuss the list on page 59.
- Understanding the five levels of communication helps us go deep with people. How familiar are you with the five levels of communication?
- Discuss each of the levels of communication using the discussion questions in the book. For example, in Level One, what clichés do we hear people use (question #3)?

✔ Practice
Break up into twos and share some information with one another (Level 2). This could include sharing about your family, living situation, current career, home, or marital status. After sharing information, discuss any common ground that people have found with one another.

   With the same conversation partner, go a little deeper. Discuss what you are learning about being an alongsider. Share some concerns or fears (Levels 3 and 4) about being an alongsider. After your conversation, discuss these two questions:
- What did you experience about the power of listening?
- What did you experience about the power of good questions?

✔ Application
Discuss together people's responses to "Alongsiders Take Action" on page 62.

✔ Leader's Review
- What level of communication does this group predominantly demonstrate?

   cliché—information—values—feelings—peak

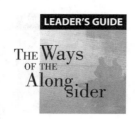

SESSION SEVEN
The Way of the Word

✔ Learning Goals

1. Describe the importance of the Scriptures in discipling another.
2. Discuss the hand illustration.
3. Practice a simple tool for meditation.

✔ Review

Discuss "An Alongsider Checkup" on page 73. Have one or two people share their timelines.

✔ Discussion

Select the questions you want to discuss:

- How would you describe the priority of God's Word in Jesus' life (question #1)?
- What did you write about the priority of God's Word in your life (see #5)?
- What did you discover about the ministry of God's Word in 2 Timothy 3:16?
- What did you discover about how to get a grip on the Bible (#6)?
- How would you assess your strengths and weaknesses in saturating your life with God's Word (#7)?
- What did you discover about the role of the Bible in truth telling?
- How comfortable are you about speaking the truth into people's lives?
- How would you describe the importance of meditating on the Word in your life?
- Review the observation-investigation-application process on page 71. How can this process help you meditate on the Word?

✔ Practice

Do the process of meditation together. Select one of these passages to meditate on as a group: Joshua 1:8; Psalm 1:1-3; 119:1-5; Colossians 3:16-17. Use the questions on page 71.

✔ Application

Ask the group, "During this next week, when is a time that you could use this meditation process? What passage of Scripture will you meditate on?"

✔ Leader's Review

- Review the VIM principle on page 72.

  ❏ Do people have a vision to love the Scriptures?
  ❏ How intentional are they about this vision?
  ❏ What means are people using?

The Way of Discovery

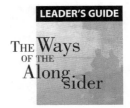

✔ Learning Goals
1. Establish the importance of personal discovery in discipling others.
2. Describe the power of good questions in being an alongsider.
3. Identify and practice the importance of making practical applications.

✔ Review
- Discuss "An Alongsider Checkup" on page 83.
- Provide time for any remaining people to share their timelines.

✔ Discussion Questions
Select the questions you want to discuss:
- What did you discover about how Jesus demonstrated a diverse teaching style?
- How do you feel about teaching being a process of discovery and not just a traditional lecture?
- Why do you think discovery is important to discipling others?
- Because Jesus was all-knowing, He did not ask questions to gain information. What do you think was His purpose in asking questions?
- What did you discover about your question-asking abilities (question #2)?
- Review each step of the Question Ladder (pages 78–79). On this ladder, what types of questions do you typically ask? What types of questions can you use more of?
- Why is a diverse set of questions important to ask as an alongsider?
- From James 1:22-25, why is doing, and not just hearing, so important (#6)?
- Review the three "Ps" on page 81. How can this approach be useful in making obedience practical?
- How can practical application enhance your attitude of obedience?

✔ Practice
Pair up with another person and pick a topic (being a friend of God, evangelism, serving people) and go up the ladder asking questions about this topic. Use the expanded list of questions on pages 78–79. Place the topic in the blank spaces of the Question Ladder. For example, how would you describe evangelism?

✔ Application
Discuss the "Alongsiders Take Action" assignment (page 82).

✔ Leader's Review
- How can you use the Question Ladder in leading the discussion in this group?

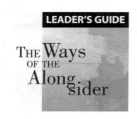
SESSION NINE

The Way of Conversation

✔ Learning Goals
1. Identify a change agent.
2. Describe what biblical change looks like.
3. Discuss the process of an alongsider conversation.

✔ Review
Discuss "An Alongsider Checkup" on page 93.

✔ Discussion
Select the questions you want to discuss:
- How do you feel about being the Holy Spirit's change agent?
- What is our role and what is God's role in the process of transformation?
- What would happen if we confused these roles?
- What did you discover about "timing"?
- Thinking in biblical time has some significant implications to the alongsider ministry. What could be some implications (question #3)?
- Why do you think conversations are a powerful tool of the Holy Spirit for change?
- Our lives are peppered with important conversations. Describe one conversation that significantly impacted your life this last year.
- How did this conversation illustrate some of the elements of an alongsider conversation?
- How have you practiced elements of an alongsider conversation?
- Why do you think each element is necessary for an alongsider conversation?
- What did you discover about the process of change from the pathway on page 90?
- Discuss how people answered #6 (page 92).

✔ Practice
As a group, choose one of the case studies on page 92. Brainstorm together how you would lead an alongsider conversation.

✔ Application
- Discuss "Alongsiders Take Action" on pages 92–93.
- Appendix G (pages 119–120) provides resources for discipling another. Review the list together.

✔ Leader's Review
- How's the weather? Assess how you're applying R + 2D + 3A (see page 129).

SESSION TEN
The Way of Mission

✔ Learning Goals
1. Understand the biblical concept of the insider.
2. Discuss the process of evangelism.
3. Establish a personal circle of influence.

✔ Review
Discuss "An Alongsider Checkup" on page 102.

✔ Discussion
Select the questions you want to discuss:
- Why do you think most church growth is by shuffling rather than conversion?
- How would you describe the growth of your church?
- We have inserted a new word in our discussion. What do think about the vision of being an "insider"?
- What did you discover about Jesus' example of the insider ministry (questions #1–2)?
- How would you describe Jesus' heart for lost people?
- How did the Apostle Paul and the early church demonstrate the power of an insider ministry (#5–6)?
- What are the distinguishing qualities of an insider ministry?
- How is this ministry similar to or different from our traditional approaches to evangelism?
- What are some simple steps we can take as insiders to reach those outside of Christ?
- Discuss your circle of influence in #8.
- How could you grow your circle of influence?
- Is thinking about evangelism as a process a new or familiar truth for you?
- How has your personal faith experience demonstrated evangelism as a process?
- Discuss your insights to questions #9–10.
- How did you answer #11?

✔ Application
Discuss answers to "An Insider Application" on pages 101–102.

✔ Leader's Review
Some of the principles in this chapter may be new to people. Take time for understanding and application.

SESSION ELEVEN
What Do I Do Next?

✔ Learning Goals

1. Capture outstanding lessons from the book.
2. Create a personal action plan of investing in an alongsider triad.

✔ Discussion

- What are one or two outstanding truths from this study that have shaped your life?
- If you were to put these truths into a sermon or message, what would you title it?

✔ Application

Walk through "An Alongsider Action Plan" together (pages 103–104).

- What do you think about the idea of recruiting a triad?
- What are the advantages of this type of small group?
- Who could you invite to this triad (review steps 1–4 on page 103)?
- A list of resources is in Appendix G, pages 119–120. What resources will help engage people firsthand in meditating on the Scriptures?

✔ Practice

Break up into twos and role-play how you will invite someone to your discipleship triad. In your invitation, describe your vision and some of the details of the group.

✔ Our Final Meeting

As an alongsider group, plan to meet in four weeks to celebrate what God has done and to share lessons you're learning about being an alongsider.

We will meet on _____ at _____.

- Stop and pray together for the establishment of several alongsider triads.

Notes

Chapter 1: The Way of the Amateur

1. Michael Green, *Evangelism in the Early Church* (Grand Rapids, MI: Eerdmans, 1976), 172–173.
2. Warren Wiersbe, *Preaching and Teaching with Imagination* (Grand Rapids, MI: Baker, 2004), 62.
3. W. E. Vine, *Vine's Expository Dictionary of New Testament Words* (McLean, VA: MacDonald Publishing Company), 400.
4. Eugene Peterson, *Practicing Resurrection* (Grand Rapids, MI: Eerdmans, 2010), 173.
5. Peterson, 175.
6. Lauren F. Winner, *Still: Notes on a Mid-Faith Crisis* (New York: HarperOne, 2012), 191.
7. Dallas Willard, *Renovation of the Heart* (Colorado Springs, CO: NavPress, 2002), 85.

Chapter 2: The Way of Life

1. John Stott, *Baptism and Fullness* (Downers Grove, IL: InterVarsity, 2006), 70.
2. Oswald Chambers, *My Utmost for His Highest* (Uhrichsville, OH: Barbour Publishing, 1965), January 6.
3. Eugene Peterson, *Living the Resurrection* (Colorado Springs, CO: NavPress, 2006), 16.
4. Ken Gire, *The Reflective Life* (Colorado Springs, CO: Chariot/Victor, 1998), 46.

Chapter 3: The Way of Intentionality

1. Bruxy Cavey, *The End of Religion* (Colorado Springs, CO: NavPress, 2007), 62.
2. Robert Coleman, *The Master Plan of Evangelism* (Old Tappan, NJ: Tappan, 1971), 108.
3. Bill Hull, *The Disciplemaking Pastor* (Old Tappan, NJ: Revell, 1988), 51.
4. Colin Brown, ed., *The New International Dictionary of New Testament Theology* (Grand Rapids, MI: Zondervan, 1980), 486–487.

Chapter 5: The Way of Relationships

1. Eugene Peterson, *Under the Unpredictable Plant* (Grand Rapids, MI: Eerdmans, 1992), 86.
2. Oswald Chambers, *My Utmost for His Highest* (Uhrichsville, OH: Barbour Publishing, 1965), November 16.
3. Robert Coleman, *The Master Plan of Evangelism* (Old Tappan, NJ: Tappan, 1971), 80.

Chapter 6: The Way of Depth

1. Philip Yancey, *Prayer: Does It Make Any Difference?* (Grand Rapids, MI: Zondervan, 2006), 41.
2. John Powell, *Why Am I Afraid to Tell You Who I Am?* (Niles, IL: Argus Communications, 1969). This is a theme throughout the book.

Chapter 7: The Way of the Word

1. Ken Gire, *The Reflective Life* (Colorado Springs, CO: Chariot/Victor, 1998), 90.

Chapter 8: The Way of Discovery

1. Dietrich Bonhoeffer, *Meditating on the Word* (Cambridge, MA: Cowley Publications, 2000), 22.
2. Philip Yancey, *Prayer: Does It Make Any Difference?* (Grand Rapids, MI: Zondervan, 2006), 205.
3. John Dear, *The Questions of Jesus* (New York: Image Books, 2004), 1.

Chapter 9: The Way of Conversation

1. Dallas Willard, *The Revolution of Character* (Colorado Springs, CO: NavPress, 2005), 18.

Chapter 10: The Way of Mission

1. An excellent source for the insider ministry is *The Insider* by Jim Petersen (Colorado Springs, CO: NavPress, 2003).

My Pledge to Be an Alongsider

1. Jim Weiker, *The Columbus Dispatch,* September 17, 2009.

Bibliography

Barna, George. *Growing True Disciples.* Colorado Springs, CO: WaterBrook, 2004.

Bonhoeffer, Dietrich. *Meditating on the Word.* Cambridge, MA: Cowley Publications, 2000.

Bounds, E. M. *Power Through Prayer.* New Kensington, PA: Whitaker House, 1982.

Cavey, Bruxy. *The End of Religion.* Colorado Springs, CO: NavPress, 2007.

Chambers, Oswald. *My Utmost for His Highest.* Uhrichsville, OH: Barbour Publishing, 1965.

Coleman, Robert E. *The Master Plan of Evangelism.* Old Tappan, NJ: Tappan, 1971.

Dear, John. *The Questions of Jesus.* New York: Image Books, 2004.

Fleming, Jean. *Feeding Your Soul.* Colorado Springs, CO: NavPress, 1999.

Foster, Richard. *Celebration of Discipline.* San Francisco: Harper, 1978.

Foster, Richard. *Prayer: Finding the Heart's True Home.* San Francisco: Harper, 1992.

Gire, Ken. *The Reflective Life.* Colorado Springs, CO: Chariot/Victor, 1998.

Green, Michael. *Evangelism in the Early Church.* Grand Rapids, MI: Eerdmans, 1976.

Hendricks, Howard G. *Teaching to Change Lives.* Portland, OR: Multnomah, 1987.

Hull, Bill. *The Disciple-Making Pastor.* Old Tappan, NJ: Revell, 1988.

Hurst, J. F. *John Wesley the Methodist.* New York: Eaton & Mains, 1903.

Johnson, Jan. *Enjoying the Presence of God.* Colorado Springs, CO: NavPress, 1996.

Johnson, Jan. *Savoring God's Word.* Colorado Springs, CO: NavPress, 2004.

Lee-Thorp, Karen. *How to Ask Great Questions.* Colorado Springs, CO: NavPress, 1998.

Lewis, C. S. *The Four Loves.* New York: Harcourt, Brace and Company, 1960.

Lyons, Gabe. *The Next Christians.* New York: Doubleday, 2010.

Matthewes-Greene, Frederica. *The Illumined Heart.* Brewster, MA: Paraclete Press, 2006.

Petersen, Jim. *Lifestyle Discipleship.* Colorado Springs, CO: NavPress, 1993.

Peterson, Eugene H. *The Contemplative Pastor.* Grand Rapids, MI: Eerdmans, 1989.

Peterson, Eugene H. *Eat This Book.* Grand Rapids, MI: Eerdmans, 2006.

Peterson, Eugene H. *Living the Resurrection.* Colorado Springs, CO: NavPress, 2006.

Peterson, Eugene H. *Practicing Resurrection.* Grand Rapids, MI: Eerdmans, 2010.

Peterson, Eugene H. *Under the Unpredictable Plant.* Grand Rapids, MI: Eerdmans, 1992.

Powell, John. *Why Am I Afraid to Tell You Who I Am?* Niles, IL: Argus Communications, 1969.

Swindoll, Charles. *Intimacy with the Almighty.* Nashville: J. Countryman, 1996.

Tozer, A. W. *The Pursuit of God.* Camp David, PA: Christian Publications, 1993.

Wiersbe, Warren. *Preaching and Teaching with Imagination.* Grand Rapids, MI: Baker, 2004.

Willard, Dallas. *The Great Omission.* San Francisco: Harper, 2006.

Willard, Dallas. *The Renovation of the Heart.* Colorado Springs, CO: NavPress, 2002.

Willard, Dallas. *The Revolution of Character.* Colorado Springs, CO: NavPress, 2005.

Willard, Dallas. *The Spirit of the Disciplines.* San Francisco: HarperCollins, 1988.

Wolff, Pierre (trans). *The Spiritual Exercises of Saint Ignatius.* Liguori, MS: Triumph, 1997.

Wright, N. T. *Surprised by Hope.* San Francisco: HarperOne, 2008.

Yancey, Philip. *Prayer: Does It Make Any Difference?* Grand Rapids, MI: Zondervan, 2006.

Zuck, Roy B. *Teaching as Jesus Taught.* Eugene, OR: Wipf & Stock, 2002.

About the Author

BILL MOWRY is a veteran staff member with The Navigators. He has discipled people in such diverse settings as a college campus, with graduate students and professors, among physicians and dentists, and with people in the workplace. Bill has an MA in adult education from The Ohio State University and is a published author in the areas of education, learning, discipleship, and leadership. He is a popular seminar leader and has brought the message of the alongsider to such places as Honduras, Bulgaria, and Singapore. Bill and his wife, Peggy, live in Columbus, Ohio, and serve with The Navigators' Church Discipleship Ministry. His passion is to create ministry cultures where people are relationally doing the Great Commission, one relationship and one conversation at a time. Bill invites you to visit his blog (BillMowry.com) and website (www.alongsider.com).

DOES YOUR CHURCH WANT TO MAKE DISCIPLES?
WE CAN HELP!

The Navigators' Church Discipleship Ministry brings a wealth of experience and resources to help pastors and churches become intentional about making disciples.

How can we help you and your church?

• We have trained coaches who can help your church make disciples through *The Ways of the Alongsider*.

• We can come to your church or community to lead The Ways of the Alongsider Coaching Clinic. For more information on our clinic, visit Alongsider.com.

• We have a time-tested process, The Intentional Disciplemaking Church Strategy, that can help your church develop a customized disciplemaking strategy. Our trained CDM coaches are positioned around the country to help your congregation become an intentional disciplemaking church.

To find out more about our coaching ministry and how we can help your church, contact us at **www.navigators.org/us/ministries/cdm**.

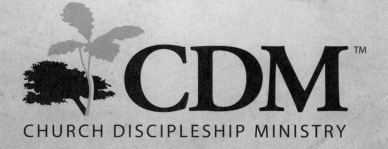

CDM™
CHURCH DISCIPLESHIP MINISTRY

4-1-14

Authentic, Transparent, Vulnerable ⟩ Just show up as we are.
Honesty, Integrity

FAT = faithful, available, teachable

Great Commission (Matt 4:19)

New Christian needs:

1) assurance of ~~salvation~~ salvation
   0 Christ in life
   2 reborn
   3 sins forgiven
   4 new relationship w/ God
   5 never be separated from God again

2) Significance of salvation
   Motivation to grow in Christ

3) Filling of H. Spirit (basic understanding)

4) Identity in Christ
   Struggle between old + new nature

5) Basic growth principle

6) Fellowship (basic understanding)

7) God's Word - How Bible is divided, begin reading on own

8) Prayer

9) Witnessing

10) Spiritual warfare (it's real)

11) Stewardship (time, talents, treasures)

12) Vision (or purpose) - understand her significance in God's plan

N A V E S S E N T I A L S

Voices of The Navigators—Past, Present, and Future

NAVESSENTIALS offer core Navigator messages from such authors as Jim Downing, LeRoy Eims, Mike Treneer, and more — at an affordable price. This new series will deeply influence generations in the movement of discipleship. Learn from the old and new messages of The Navigators how powerful and transformational the life of a disciple truly is.

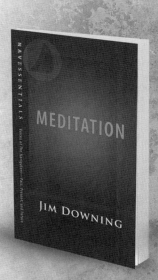

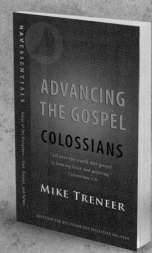

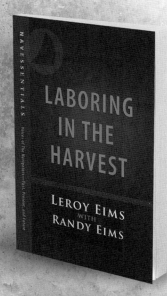

Meditation
by Jim Downing
9781615217250 | $5.00

Advancing the Gospel
by Mike Treneer
9781617471575 | $5.00

Laboring in the Harvest
by LeRoy Eims with Randy Eims
9781615216406 | $10.99

To order, go to **www.NavPress.com** or call **1-800-366-7788**.

NAVPRESS
Discipleship Inside Out®

The Message Means Understanding

Bringing the Bible to all ages

The Message is written in contemporary language that is much like talking with a good friend. When paired with your favorite Bible study, *The Message* will deliver a reading experience that is reliable, energetic, and amazingly fresh.

To find *The Message* that is right for you, go to **www.navpress.com** or call **1-800-366-7788**.

NAVPRESS
Discipleship Inside Out®

NavPress - A Ministry of The Navigators

*Wherever you are in your spiritual journey,
NavPress will help you grow.*

The NavPress mission is to advance the calling of The Navigators by publishing life-transforming products that are biblically rooted, culturally relevant, and highly practical.

www.NavPress.com   1-800-366-7788

NAVPRESS
Discipleship Inside Out®